Dancing with the Energy

Book 1:
The Foundations of Conscious Living

Dennis L. Dossett, PhD

Dancing with the Energy
Book 1: The Foundations of Conscious Living

**Copyright © 2020
by Dennis L. Dossett**
www.DennisDossett.com

All rights reserved. No part of this publication, either in part or in whole, may be reproduced, transmitted or utilized in any form, by any means, electronic, photographic, or mechanical, including photocopying, recording or by any information storage system, without permission in writing from the author, except for brief quotations embodied in literary articles and reviews.

Cover design by Dennis L. Dossett

Shiva, the Hindu god of Destruction, Rebirth, Transformation, and Change blends with the vast infinity of the Cosmos as he dances his way through space, time, and the human experience.

All rights reserved.

Suite 300 - 990 Fort St
Victoria, BC, V8V 3K2
Canada

www.friesenpress.com

Library of Congress Control Number available on request

ISBN
978-1-5255-6268-6 (Hardcover)
978-1-5255-6269-3 (Paperback)
978-1-5255-6270-9 (eBook)

1. BODY, MIND & SPIRIT, INSPIRATION & PERSONAL GROWTH

Distributed to the trade by The Ingram Book Company

Printed in the United States of America

Dedication:
Margaret McElroy
(1946-2016)

In honor of her life's work and passion, this series of books is dedicated to my dear friend and mentor, Margaret McElroy, spiritual intuitive, counselor, and deep-trance channel for the Spirit teacher known as Maitreya. Without Margaret's steadfast guidance and bringing Maitreya and his teachings to the world, these books would not have been possible.

Margaret began teaching about the world of Spirit in 1987. Maitreya formally introduced himself to the world on June 8, 1999 in a channeling at a meeting of SEAT, the Society for Enlightenment and Transformation. SEAT is a group within the United Nations in New York City under the United Nations Staff Recreational Council.

Margaret left an incredible legacy of teachings and writings from her teacher, Maitreya. She traveled the world with Maitreya, allowing him the ability to channel and to teach thousands of people at both public and private events as well as through the Maitreya website. He trained many teachers to carry forward his message and left his website (www.Maitreya.co) as the repository for his writings.

Maitreya often referred to his "missives" (as he called them) as "Wisdom for Today, Answers for Tomorrow," a means of helping people to understand their life circumstances as they navigate their way through the world around them. The wisdom in these writings—as well as audio and video recordings—is a gift to all those who are drawn to Maitreya's message of becoming the Master of your own life. The content is timeless and focuses on YOU taking ownership of your life and facing your fears by learning the life lessons you have chosen through the context of your astrology, karma, and past life energy.

Table of Contents

Preface and Acknowledgments ix

Introduction to Book 1: The Foundations of Conscious Living .. xv

Chapter 1: The Purpose of Life 1
- Soul Evolution 1
- Self and Higher Self 2
- Levels of Human Consciousness or Awareness 5
- Raising Your Consciousness 12
- Summary of Raising Your Consciousness 14
- Conscious Living 15

Chapter 2: It's All About the Energy! 17
- Quality of Energy 19
- General Principles of Dancing with the Energy 22
- Tips for Allowing the Energy to Flow 31
- Summary of General Energy Principles 34
- Thoughts are Energy! 35
- Emotions are Energy! 36
- The Soul Itself is Energy! 36
- Summary of Energy Principles and Tips for Allowing 37
- Conscious Living and Energy 38

Chapter 3: Human Energy Fields and the Ancient Wisdoms 39
- Introduction 39
- The Subtle Bodies 41
- Comments on the Subtle Bodies 46
- Controlling the Energy Fields 52
- The Chakras 54
- Conscious Living and the Ancient Wisdoms 62

Chapter 4: Human Energy Fields and Quantum Physics 63
    Introduction 63
    The Basic Precepts of Quantum Physics 63
    Quantum Physics and the Ancient Wisdoms 79
    Changing Behaviors and Habits 80
    Summary of Human Energy Fields and Quantum Physics 83
    Conscious Living and Quantum Physics 84

Chapter 5: The Power of Your Thoughts 85
    Introduction 85
    Conscious Thoughts 86
    Beliefs 88
    Tips for Effectively Utilizing Your Thoughts 92
    Summary of Tips for Effectively Utilizing Your Thoughts 100
    Conscious Living and Thoughts 100

Chapter 6: Managing Your Emotions 101
    Introduction 101
    Emotions and Emotional States 102
    Emotions and Conscious Living 106
    Your Vibrational Indicator 110
    Tips for Working with Your Emotions 113
    Summary of Tips for Working with Your Emotions 119
    Conscious Living and Emotions 119

Chapter 7: The Conscious and Subconscious Minds 121
    Introduction 121
    Conscious and Subconscious Relationships 127
    Dealing with Unexpressed or Unused Energy 131
    Tips for Dealing with Subconscious Emotions 135
    Habits and the Subconscious Mind 139
    Tips for Changing Your Habits 143
    Summary of Tips for Conscious & Subconscious Minds 148
    Conscious Living and the Subconscious Mind 149

Chapter 8: Understanding Conscious Living 151
    Introduction 151
    Unconscious Living 151
    Conscious Living 152
    General Tips for Creating Conscious Living 153
    Dynamic Balance 158
    Tips for Achieving Dynamic Balance 163
    Summary of Tips for Conscious Living 166

Concluding Comments 167

Contents of Book 2: Conscious Living — What's Holding You Back? 169

Contents of Book 3: Conscious Living — Creating the Life You Desire 169

Appendix A: Inspirational and Educational Resources 171

vii

Preface and Acknowledgments

Dancing with the Energy is about transforming <u>your</u> life, changing the energies of <u>your</u> life—physical, mental, emotional, and etheric—for the purpose of soul evolution. It is about learning how to consciously take charge of your life in order to improve its quality and to create the life *you want*. It is also about the transformation from fear to fearlessness. You will learn a good deal more about these energies and how to transform them in the three books in this series.

The primary message of **Conscious Living** is one of taking responsibility for one's entire life—past (including past lives), present, and future. That is not a message for the faint-hearted, and thus many potential readers are likely to stop reading at the end of this sentence. But I believe in 'truth in packaging.'

With self-responsibility comes the obligation for personal growth. I believe *everything* in life—the good, the bad, the beautiful, the ugly—is for *one purpose*. That purpose is to provide each of us with an *opportunity* to take a step—to grow—into becoming a better version of ourselves; in other words, soul evolution. The theme of this series of books is thus focused on *growth* and *progress* with practical Tips for how to manifest these objectives in one's daily life.

The fact is, I wrote the ***Dancing with the Energy*** books to better inform myself about how to accomplish exactly these objectives. I have relied on the convergence of writings from the Ancient Wisdoms to Nobel Laureates in Physics, from spiritual masters and teachers to the observations and experiences of the captains of industry as well as common people on the street. For over four decades I have told my students that "Wisdom has nothing to do with who said it, but whether it helps you to grow." I still believe that, and wherever I found different perspectives converging on the same concepts and methods, I found confidence in their recommendations and have shared them in these books.

In the process of writing, I discovered both major points and nuances of *Conscious Living* of which at the outset I was either only vaguely aware or I mistakenly thought I completely understood. To say that this project has been an education is a gross understatement. As a result, I have grown immensely both in my own understanding and in the practical application of the principles of *Conscious Living* in my own life. I will be forever grateful to Spirit, both for the wonderful education and for the opportunity to write these books for the benefit of those who may find them helpful in their own lives.

Not all of the ideas in these books are new. The integration of seemingly different perspectives so they fit into a comprehensive, understandable package for guiding one's life and the practical steps for implementing them are my contribution. But the credit ultimately belongs to Spirit, for I am just a student. However, I accept full responsibility for everything contained in these pages as *the best of my understanding at this point in my own soul evolution.*

As is each of us, I am an evolutionary work in progress and, in that spirit, I invite the reader to join me on our own respective journeys. As I have written elsewhere, "We are all on different paths together, eventually ending up at the same destination in our own good time and in our own chosen way." *Dancing with the Energy* of *Conscious Living* is only one way, but not a bad starting point for those who consciously desire not only to improve the quality of their life right here and now, but also to raise their vibration—to further their soul evolution.

- "The further the spiritual evolution of mankind advances, the more certain it seems to me that the path to genuine religiosity does not lie through the fear of life, and the fear of death, and blind faith, but through striving after rational knowledge." ~ attributed to Albert Einstein

Personal growth is a gradual, step-by-step process requiring a plan, dedication, and hard work. As I have said to many of my clients and students over the years, "Old habits die hard, but with a little faith and a lot of hard work, they die before you do!"

The genesis of these books was an 83-week internet radio show entitled "The Energies of Your Life," co-hosted with Jean Luo, my long-time colleague and dear friend. It was Jean who introduced me to the term *Dancing with the Energy* late in that series and which later became the main title for the three books. For us, the radio show was an enlightening foundation for our respective journeys into *Conscious Living*. We started out with the goal of spiritual teaching—metaphysical education. As the number of weekly shows grew, we found ourselves grappling with our own life lessons of which we became increasingly aware. As the old saying goes, "If you really want to understand something, try to teach it to others." Thank you, Jean, for your wonderful friendship, advice, and insightful contributions to many of the ideas in this these books. You have been an inspiration both personally and professionally, and you have been a profoundly positive influence in my life.

I also want to thank my friend and mentor, Margaret McElroy, spiritual intuitive, counselor, and deep-trance channel for the energy known as Maitreya. Without Margaret's steadfast guidance and bringing Maitreya and his teachings to the world, my own spiritual understanding and these books would not have been possible. References to Maitreya's teachings in these books were channeled by Margaret. Together, their contributions to spiritual understanding have greatly enriched the lives of countless millions of souls on the earth plane.

In addition, my dear friend and spiritual mentor, Alan McElroy, provided the time, the technology, and the means for the internet radio shows that became the basis for much of the content of these books. Thank you, Alan. I could not have traveled as far on my own spiritual journey without your guidance and support. Your unwavering friendship has only deepened over the years and is very much appreciated.

I also want to acknowledge the advice of another friend and mentor in this as well as in past lives, Jon Martin Anastasio. His insight and feedback on early drafts were instrumental in creating and improving the entire series of *Dancing with the Energy* books. His experience as a published author and his guidance are evident in the final product. For encouraging me and helping me to make this work even more readable, thank you, Jon.

Preface and Acknowledgments

To my marvelous editor, Linda Zeppa, my readers and I thank you for correcting my errors, clarifying my intent, and making these books much more readable. You are the best!

Finally, I am so deeply indebted and grateful to my wonderful wife and life partner, Karen Dossett. She and I broadcast another series of nearly 30 weekly internet radio shows that also contributed greatly to the content of these books. Her patient editing and re-editing, along with frequent challenges to 'simplify' in order to better communicate my intended thoughts to potential readers immeasurably enhanced the quality and readability of these books. Her steadfast encouragement and loving perspective also made writing them much easier for me. Karen, you have made me a better man, a better father, and a better human being through your untiring love. I am truly blessed to have you as the love of my life. Thank you so very, very much!

Dennis L. Dossett

Introduction to Book 1: The Foundations of Conscious Living

Dancing with the Energy is about the process of becoming the Master of your life, raising your vibration, and creating the life you desire. This process is called **Conscious Living** and it is the key to manifesting those objectives. It is very much like building a house:

- First, you have to *prepare for the work* by creating a plan—a blueprint—and by assessing available raw materials (lumber, nails, pipes, electrical wiring, etc.) and gathering tools (saw, hammer, tape measure, etc.) along with the knowledge and skill to put them all together.

- Second, you have to *understand and follow the rules*, the constraints and requirements (zoning laws, building and construction permits, safety & building inspections, etc.) that must be met in order to begin and to complete the construction process.

- Third is the actual construction, *doing the work*. The house begins to take shape using the tools and raw materials in the most effective and efficient manner possible (building and construction techniques, etc.)—within the limits of the *constraints* and *requirements*.

Becoming the Master of your life, raising your vibration, and creating the life you desire follow the same basic steps outlined above. All three are critically important and must be followed largely in that order if you expect to actually complete the construction process. That process is the topic of **Dancing with the Energy.**

Everyone is born with the basic raw materials and tools for living, but relatively few individuals know how to apply those tools most effectively to the raw materials. Even fewer have a consistent, overall plan for constructing their lives. Beyond choosing a means of making a living (job, profession, career, etc.) and wandering through a maze of relationships hoping to find one that 'works,' life just seems to 'happen' to many people rather than unfold according to a plan they have consciously chosen as a means of creating a healthy and satisfying life. That is where **Conscious Living** comes into play, so let's begin at the beginning.

Book 1: The Foundations of Conscious Living is the first in a series of three books. It is the precursor to understanding and implementing what it takes to improve the quality of your life here and now, as well as in the future. It all begins with understanding the Foundations, the plan and the basic materials available to you for creating (manifesting) the life you desire, as well as understanding the tools you have at your disposal and how to use them most effectively. Without both understanding the plan and developing skill in applying your inherent tools effectively, you will quickly find yourself 'stuck' repeatedly throughout your life. But with a little practice and learning to constantly

Introduction to Book 1: The Foundations of Conscious Living

monitor *how* you live your life, you can begin to move into the next phases of constructing your life according to the plan you choose.

Books 2 and 3 in the *Dancing with the Energy* series will take you into the next steps in the process of successful living, but they require that you first understand, practice, and develop a degree of mastery in the *Foundations of Conscious Living*.

*Note: Superscripted$^{Bx, Cy}$ notations in this book refer to **Book x, Chapter y** in the *Dancing with the Energy* series.

Chapter 1: The Purpose of Life

Soul Evolution

The purpose of life on the earth plane is soul evolution. The end goal of soul evolution is eventually merging with the consciousness of the Ultimate Being, Tao, God, Source—whatever you wish to call that energy. And that energy has been described almost uniformly across cultures and millennia as complete, unconditional love.

Other terms for soul evolution are: transformation, raising your vibration, moving forward in consciousness, enlightenment, ascension, etc. ***Transformation*** is the ***change in consciousness*** as you ***learn through experience*** and ***grow*** into higher levels of consciousness, in other words, soul evolution. It is all about changing the energies of your life—physical, mental, emotional, and etheric—for the purpose of becoming a better version of yourself.

Soul evolution is a gradual process, taking many years in one lifetime and also many lifetimes. The earth plane is a schoolhouse where we have an opportunity to learn and grow—to evolve—through our life experiences. As the old saying goes, "Life is a school and class is always in session."

- "You have come to the earth plane to attend school. Yes, even though you are adults, the earth plane is a school, and there are classrooms and teachers. Each classroom is a lesson. Instead of mathematics and English, science and sports, the lessons in this school are patience, letting go of fear, understanding, compassion, etc. You are all students learning about life itself and how to play the game, for life is a game and, once you learn how to play that game, life becomes a lot easier to live." ~ Maitreya (Newsletter #355, June 1, 2011)

Self and Higher Self

When people write or speak about 'growing into higher levels of consciousness,' what do they mean? To understand that, one first has to understand the concepts of ***Self*** and ***Higher Self***.

The ***Self*** (sometimes referred to as the ***Lower Self***) is basically the ***survival instinct.*** Maitreya identified the Self as playing the role of 'the Devil' in people's lives. Paramhansa Yogananda (1893–1952; yogi and spiritual teacher) called it the 'Satan' of the *Bible,* and it exists only on the earth plane. Both of them speak of it as a *conscious energy* with only one purpose—to maintain its own existence and power. It needs energy to survive, and does so by 'feeding' on negative emotions (for example, doubt, fear, anger, etc.).

The Self masquerades as your 'protector' (survival instinct), preferring habit and the comfort zone to change and growth because they subtly lull you into 'going along' with the Self's own desires and needs. It knows you better than you know yourself because it has instant and more complete access to your subconscious mind than you do. In order to maintain its existence, the Self works to control you by magnifying negative emotions. As a conscious force, it knows that, when you initiate change in your life, it has to use all of its resources to fight back or lose its control. As a result, it stops you from growing, transforming, and raising your level of consciousness.

A related, but separate concept is the ***Ego***. The Ego is essentially your self-identity. The Self uses the Ego for its own purposes, which are to feed on and strengthen itself on negativity, especially fear and doubt, both major components of self-esteem and self-worth. Too much or too little either way creates imbalance. The Ego has to be ***Balanced*** or the transformation of consciousness from Self to Higher Self cannot occur. The whole purpose of life on the earth plane is to find that balance, and that is when you begin to get control of the Self.

The ***Higher Self*** is basically your direct soul connection with Source Energy, the Ultimate Being, God—whatever you wish to call that energy. It is what you are growing toward and what you most identify with when you return to the world of Spirit.

To compare these concepts a bit, the ***Lower Self*** operates through pride, selfishness, greed, ego, fear, hatred, and many more negative emotions. In contrast, the ***Higher Self*** supports love, truth, selflessness, honesty, compassion, understanding, non-prejudice, and many more positive qualities. Soul evolution is the gradual process of transforming your consciousness from Self to Higher Self through learning and life experience.

The Ego (as self-identity) is also your sense of separateness from everything else—including the Higher Self which is your direct connection to Source Energy or the Ultimate Being,

God. Yogananda defined the Ego as "the Soul identified with the body."

When you live primarily in the energy of the Higher Self, the Ego becomes less and less relevant. Getting to this point is a lengthy process of transformation characterized by a battle between the Lower Self and the Higher Self that culminates in what is called "Cosmic Consciousness." The Higher Self is the part of you that is becoming enlightened, but the Lower Self does not want to give up control. In this battle, ego purification (**Balance**) *has* to take place, and finally the Ego—the 'I' part of you that does not want to give in—finally succumbs to defeat (becomes '*purified*' or '*Balanced*'). Only then, can the soul find true enlightenment and become one with the Divine Source.

The most important teachers in my life—Maitreya, Abraham, and Yogananda—all agree that relationships of all types provide one of the most important vehicles for growth and transformation on the earth plane. This includes the relationships among the various parts or energies of ourselves. For example:

- "Humankind are now learning of the relationship between the body, mind and Soul [Higher Self]. It is very important that this be learned because only when all three are in **balance** can a person find peace within themselves and have 'a peace that passes all understanding.'" ~ Maitreya ("The New Millennium")

Most importantly, each of these teachers is clear that the single, most important relationship in your life is with your Higher Self. It is your true essence as Spirit, the 'real you' aside from all the trappings and limitations of life in your physical body. As we shall discuss in Chapter 2 (and throughout the *Dancing with the Energy* books), your life is all about growing into greater **Alignment** with your Higher Self through the **Balancing** of *all of* your life energies. *Dancing with the Energy* is all about **Conscious Living** and learning how to balance these energies to improve the quality of your daily life and to become the Master of your life.

Levels of Human Consciousness or Awareness

As stated above, the process of 'enlightenment' is another term for 'soul evolution.' This process involves a series of stages or levels of soul evolution, which can be characterized as follows:

1. – MASS CONSCIOUSNESS OR BASE ENERGY

This stage includes the vast majority of people on the planet. In this stage one has little or no interest in, or even awareness of, the soul or the Higher Self. Most people at this level of consciousness simply exist day to day and are found in both less and more 'advanced' civilizations.

2. – LUNAR CONSCIOUSNESS

When you first begin to raise your vibration, you enter Lunar Consciousness. This stage is reached when a person decides they want to find out more about life and its meaning, often through religion or metaphysics. At this stage one may even start to develop clairvoyant and healing ability and become more sensitive.

3. – *SOLAR CONSCIOUSNESS*

In this stage, one begins to feel more confident in their knowledge of life and may even teach others. For example, they might teach a yoga class or a Sunday School class, or even teach astrology. They become even more attuned to spirituality and start to heal and clear problems from their subtle bodies.[B1, C3] Each of us not only has a physical body, but emotional (or astral), mental, and spiritual bodies as well. In Solar Consciousness, one begins to clear the energy blocks from these areas.

4. – *STELLAR CONSCIOUSNESS*

In this step, you still live in the illusion of the earth plane, but you begin to face your fears and doubts (the Self) that have built up over hundreds—even thousands—of past lives. Facing your fears becomes a conscious choice at this stage of soul evolution.

Stellar Consciousness is also the point of no return in spiritual development. You can't go back to an earlier stage because you know too much, and you can't 'unlearn' what you already know. 'You can run but you can't hide,' so the choice is either to progress by facing your fears, learning your unlearned lessons, and **Balancing** your karma, or else to stagnate at this level until you consciously decide to raise your vibration and get on with the process of soul evolution.

Very few people are able to work completely through this level of consciousness in one lifetime. Consequently, most people in this stage are likely to remain at this level for the remainder of their current incarnation.

5. – *Cosmic Consciousness*

Cosmic Consciousness is very difficult because the Self fights with all its strength to stay in control. During this stage of soul evolution, you become increasingly aware of the illusion of the Earth plane, you become acutely aware of what the Self is and how it operates, and you consciously work to live less and less under the control of the Self. This allows you to begin to live an increasingly greater percentage of daily life under the primary influence of the Higher Self.

During this stage, get used to feeling lonely, discouraged, worthless, guilty, ashamed, full of regret, etc. This is the Self, and it is in a battle for survival. This battle between the Self/Ego and the Higher Self occurs entirely within one's own consciousness. This stage is well-documented (often at a very symbolic and/or allegorical level) in the literature of various religions and cultures. For example:

- The Essene *War Scroll*, one of the Dead Sea scrolls discovered in a cave of the Wadi Qumran in the Judean desert, describes the apocalyptic battle between the "Sons of Light" and the "Sons of Darkness"—basically good versus evil.

- Similarly, the Hindu *Mahabharata* and the *Bhagavad Gita* describe the epic battle between the Kaurava princes (our dark/evil aspects) and the Pandava princes (our light/good aspects) on the plains of Kurukshetra in ancient India. While the story is about the triumph of light over darkness, good over evil, at the individual level it also represents the battle between the Self/Ego and the Higher Self.

- St. John of the Cross was a 16th century Roman Catholic priest who wrote the spiritual classic, *The Dark Night of the*

Soul, while imprisoned by the Church during the Spanish Inquisition. Unlike the two previous examples which symbolically portray the level of Cosmic Consciousness, St. John gives his personal account of his battle between the Self/Ego and the Higher Self.

6. – *Universal Consciousness*

This is the final stage of consciousness attainable on the earth plane, but it includes only those who are working on a very high level of cooperation with the spiritual realms. To reach Universal Consciousness means that you have finally learned your life lessons[B2, C3], dealt with your karma[B2, C4], cleared your past-life energy blockages[B2, C5], and you are a clear channel for Spirit. Merging with the Divine Force, God, Ultimate Being, or whatever you wish to call that superior energy is the next step. It is available only to the greatest spiritual teachers.

Universal Consciousness is the level at which one regularly experiences the "peace that passes understanding" spoken of in various world scriptures. In this level one is still living *on* the earth plane in a human body but their consciousness is no longer *of* the earth plane. They identify (that is, *feel*) themselves as the Higher Self. In Universal Consciousness one experiences the full import of this statement most of the time in daily life, even though the Self is still present.

- "The peace that surpasses all understanding can only come when one has reached a certain level of vibration, when the Self is controlled, and when one has worked through all old programmed negative energy. One cannot have peace if one is plagued by doubt, fear, insecurity, jealousy, anger, and other emotional feelings. Once these feelings are no longer there, then there is so much space for love and for peace in one's life. The purpose of the Self is to stop you from having this peace, to involve you in the actions of another and not in your own issues, and so it keeps you occupied all of the time. There is no time for meditation, no time for prayer, no time for happiness.

"The Self is the treadmill and you allow yourselves to be on that wheel. You have an expression on the earth plane, 'Take time to smell the roses.' The Self does not want to smell the roses; it wants to do other things. While the Self is there—driving you and fooling you—you cannot find peace under any circumstance. *The peace that surpasses all understanding is a situation of detachment [non-attachment], where no one mirrors for you anymore, nothing concerns you, and you have no fear. All that you need manifests when you think of it.* It is truly 'Heaven on Earth.' All souls can attain to this level of vibration; it is not limited to a few souls. ALL souls can reach this level of consciousness, but only after going through the battle between the Self and the Higher Self. When one does this, one is truly one with God." ~ Maitreya (Newsletter #159, July 31, 2005)

PROGRESSION THROUGH THE STAGES OF CONSCIOUSNESS

There is rarely a sharp demarcation between one level of consciousness and the next. In most cases an individual will have 'one foot' in Lunar Consciousness, for example, and 'another foot' in Solar Consciousness for a few months or even for several years. Progress is gradual, and patience with yourself can be very helpful. If you have little patience, you will certainly learn to develop it on the spiritual path!

Spiritual growth or transformation is not a chronological process in which you proceed in linear fashion from one stage to another on a given schedule. Human beings grow or mature at different rates in different parts of their lives depending on many different factors. You will find yourself being pulled in different directions simultaneously, sometimes by your desires for the future, sometimes by the opportunities and constraints in your life right now, but always by the degree to which you allow your past (especially past lives) to dictate the limits of your experience and progress.

Soul evolution involves both awareness (experience-based knowledge) and readiness (motivation x timing). Awareness is a necessary but not sufficient condition for raising your consciousness beyond a certain point and, of course, you must be ready for the next step of soul evolution to occur. Thus, there is no set amount of time an individual will spend in any of these stages; it is entirely up to the soul's desire and its readiness. Most souls have been mired in Base Consciousness for thousands of lifetimes, but that's okay. Every soul is exactly where it needs to be for its current level of soul evolution.

The amount of time one spends in a given stage from Lunar Consciousness through Cosmic Consciousness varies quite a bit from one individual to the next. A person who is seriously committed to raising their level of consciousness as quickly as possible could reasonably expect to be in a given stage between five and eight years, again depending on how they respond to the challenges of learning and releasing old energy. The main objective of the books in the *Dancing with the Energy* series is to assist with this process. It will take a little more or a little less time, depending on the individual soul's readiness and determination to detach from the Self and willingly submit or 'surrender' to the Higher Self.

- "Many people ask me, 'Why can't spiritual development happen more quickly than it does?' We in Spirit wish that this could be so, but it needs to happen slowly because if not, your physical bodies would not be able to handle the energy. As one raises the vibration of one's body, this has an effect on the whole glandular/hormonal system. It affects each one of the chakras and starts the process of release of all negative energy within the soul system." ~ Maitreya (Newsletter #60, November 25, 2002)

The percentage of those who actively continue to progress drops almost exponentially at each stage of soul evolution. Many people never go any higher in their current life because the Self holds them at a given level through fear and self-doubt. Some people do well to advance one or two steps in a given lifetime, but those who are seriously committed to raising their level of consciousness and continue on in their spiritual development can make slow but steady progress by engaging in what I call '*Conscious Living*.' I will discuss this in greater detail.[B1, C8; B2, C1]

Get used to the fact that you (I, *all* of us) are a 'work in progress.' The destination must always be kept foremost, but the daily experience is all about progress, about *becoming* a better version of yourself. This requires *consciously directed change* (*Conscious Living*). When you decide that the comfort zone—the *status quo*—is where you want to stay, you stop further progress in life. This is a kind of 'death sentence' to which most people unconsciously submit themselves.

The consciousness level of nations, cultures, and indeed the planet reflects the consciousness of their individual members or inhabitants. Looking back over history, one can see the slow but steady rise in the level of consciousness in mankind. History (both ancient and recent) indicates that the human species has a long way yet to go, but we are getting there, one soul at a time. Ultimately, the pace of progress for the planet as a whole is still an individual choice.

Every soul on the earth plane is on the path from the moment they are born until they die and decide to be reborn again into a physical body. Soul evolution is a continuous process of learning, whether we are in the world of Spirit or are living in a physical body on the earth plane. We are all at different stages of awareness and have different degrees of motivation to raise our level of consciousness.

Raising Your Consciousness

What does it take to raise your consciousness and become the Master of your life? There are three parts to this question, and each one is important to the overall process. They are separate, but not necessarily independent, and they aren't dealt with in any particular order. Sometimes you work on one for a while and then interrupt the process to work on another or even all of them at once. It is a matter of individual readiness, timing, and (most of all) *choice*. Each part involves **Balancing** the energy you carry forward through the process of soul evolution, a concept I will discuss in greater detail in Chapter 2.

#1 Learning Your Life Lessons

The first aspect of raising your consciousness is learning your life lessons.[B2, C3] Before you incarnated in this lifetime, you chose (in consultation with your Guardian Spirit, guides, and other souls) the, as yet, unlearned lessons you would attempt to master in your upcoming life. A lesson involves something special you have chosen to learn (for example, patience, letting go of fear, etc.).

Keep in mind that, when we are in Spirit, we tend to be pretty ambitious about what we want to accomplish in the next life. Once we arrive here on Earth and get mired down in the details of daily living, however, we often lose our enthusiasm and commitment—usually due to fear. Life on the earth plane is not as easy as it appears to us from the other side because we do not have a Self when we are in the world of Spirit. Whether we actually carry through with the planned lessons is a matter of choice moment-by-moment and, due to the Self, we often choose to turn and run away or hide from our lessons rather than face them.

#2 BALANCING YOUR KARMIC OBLIGATIONS

The second aspect of raising your consciousness involves karma. Karma is generated by your thoughts, words, and deeds. If you think, speak, and act positively, you create—and will experience—harmony with your Higher Self. If you think, speak, and act negatively, you will create and experience disharmony or imbalance in the soul energy that is YOU (your Higher Self). For every action there is a reaction (***Balance***). The soul knows when it has stepped over the boundary and a karmic imbalance is incurred even when your conscious mind does not. It is all about soul evolution.

Karma *always* involves one or more lessons to be learned. Why? Because, if you had already learned the lesson, you would have chosen to behave differently rather than generate additional karmic imbalance. I will have more to say about this topic later.

B2, C4

#3 *Releasing Past-Life Energy*

The underlying premise of past lives is the continuity of life. 'Death,' as you call it, is simply a transitional state between 'life' on the earth plane and life in Spirit. The transition from Spirit to the earth plane you call 'conception and birth.' You are 'born' into a new body that eventually 'dies,' but you are not the body. You are Spirit, temporarily incarnated into a physical body for the purpose of using your physical experience as a tool to stimulate and facilitate your soul evolution.

In this life, you are the accumulated total of all of your past lives. All the lessons learned and unlearned, all the accumulated karma that has not been **Balanced**, all of the trapped emotional energy (for example, anger, fear, unworthiness, etc.) which has not yet been released or healed is stored in your soul's energy field.[B1, C3, C4]

Emotion is energy, and if it is not expressed, it becomes a problem, not only in this life, but often in many incarnations to come. If past-life or other trapped energy is not cleared, it can manifest as mental and/or physical illness or other health problems. I will discuss past-life energy and its release in greater detail later.[B2, C5]

Summary of Raising Your Consciousness

- #1 Learning Your Life Lessons
- #2 Balancing Karmic Obligations
- #3 Releasing Past-Life Energy

Chapter 1: The Purpose of Life

Conscious Living

Soul evolution can occur much faster if you *consciously attune yourself to the higher spiritual energies.* That is a process I call *Conscious Living*, which I will describe later in greater detail.[B1, C8; B2, C1] In essence, it is the 'fast-track' to spiritual development and soul evolution, and I will provide specific tips to help you to learn how to engage in *Conscious Living* throughout the course of the *Dancing with the* Energy books.

"Before you are born you choose to fulfill the learning of lessons, to *Balance* karma, and to work through relationships. However, *many of you are not aware that all of that can change because of the choices you make.*" ~ Maitreya (Newsletter #221, February 24, 2009)

Chapter 2:
It's All About the Energy!

In 1905, one of the greatest physicists of the 20th century, Albert Einstein (1879–1955; physicist, 1921 Nobel Prize in Physics), published the most famous mathematical equation in history, $E = mc^2$ (energy equals mass multiplied by square of the speed of light). In other words, a given amount of matter (mass) multiplied by a very, very large number (the speed of light squared) produces an incredible amount of energy. Conversely, it takes an incredible amount of energy to produce a relatively small amount of matter. Einstein's formula tells us that **matter and energy are transposable**, so all matter is converted from energy, and matter can be converted back into energy. Neither matter nor energy can be created nor destroyed, only converted from one to the other.

By the end of the 20th century, many of the brightest minds in physics (as well as other sciences) were beginning to speculate that even consciousness itself is energy, something that metaphysicists have been saying for centuries! And while metaphysics is often presented as a 'New Age' topic, it actually goes back several millennia to the 'Ancient Wisdoms' as they are often called.[B1, C3] Today, more and more scientists and spiritual writers alike are adopting quantum physics[B1, C4] as a basis not only for understanding physical matter and energy, but also for understanding the energy of consciousness. Both ancient and modern perspectives provide useful and practical ways to understand our world—and our place in it—as well as our relationship to the world of Spirit. Thus, *"From the Ancient Wisdoms to Quantum Physics, It's All About the Energy!"*

Energy is just energy. Energy is neither positive nor negative; it just *IS*. There is a tendency (especially in metaphysical circles) to refer to 'good' energy versus 'bad' energy, or 'positive energy' versus 'negative energy,' but these terms can be very misleading and are often not very helpful in a practical sense. 'Energy' as typically thought of on the earth plane is primarily measured by its *frequency*, the rate at which something is vibrating. In the previous chapter, I discussed 'raising your vibration,' which sounds a great deal as if I were talking about raising the numeric frequency of your vibration. However, you need to be very clear regarding the difference between *quantity vs. quality of energy* in your thinking.

Consider the frequencies of sound for example. The lower the frequency, the lower the tone or pitch of a musical note. If you compare soul evolution (raising your vibration) to sound, some people might conclude that listening to higher-pitched musical notes would help them to raise their vibration, while listening to music in a lower register could actually retard their spiritual growth. If that were the case, why is it that a high-pitched scream is generally regarded as 'bad,' while the extremely low sounds of baleen whales (which they use to communicate with each other over very long distances under water) are regarded by many people as some of the most beautiful and transcendent sounds they have ever heard?

And what about the frequencies of visible light? Red light has a lower frequency (425 terahertz, energy level = 1.77 electron volts) than the color violet (714 terahertz, energy level = 2.95 electron volts) at the other end of the visible light spectrum. Does that make violet 'good' and red 'bad?' Or does it make violet 'better' than red? Or in terms of just one practical application, is the crown chakra (violet) 'better' or 'more desirable' than the base chakra (red)? If you understand anything about chakras[B1, C3], your answer certainly would be "NO!" Clearly, the answers to these questions are just not that simplistic.

These are just two examples of energy frequencies that can be quantitatively measured by physicists. But what about the frequencies of energy in the non-physical world of Spirit? What does it really mean to 'raise your vibration' in terms of 'energy?'

Quality of Energy

The answer to that question is that I am talking about energy from an entirely different perspective. 'Soul evolution' cannot be measured quantitatively on the earth plane. Rather, the levels of human consciousness or awareness[B1, C1] are ***qualitatively different*** from each other. 'Raising your vibration' (your level of consciousness) changes the fundamental nature of who you are as a spiritual being having a human experience. ***Your level of spiritual awareness is a qualitative indicator of how closely you live your life from moment to moment in terms of Alignment with your Higher Self.***

From the standpoint of soul evolution, raising your vibration from one level to the next is certainly desirable, but it doesn't by any means indicate that a person at a 'higher level' of soul evolution is 'better' than a person at a 'lower level.' We are all more advanced in some areas of spiritual development and less advanced in others, and we all have our individual lessons, karma, and unfinished business to take care of. That is why each of us is here on the earth plane.

There is a qualitative aspect to energy that I should mention here and will refer to frequently in subsequent chapters of the *Dancing with the Energy* books. You are likely to hear some people refer to a situation (for example, a house, a musical selection, an object, a particular person) as having 'bad energy,' or a different situation as having a 'high vibration.' What people are actually referring to is **how they respond** to such situations in a manner **they believe is consistent with spiritual awareness**. In other words, they have formed a **judgment**, a topic discussed in more detail in later chapters. It would be much better to avoid judging events, objects, or people[B2, C1] and simply say that **'the situation** (whatever it is) **doesn't resonate with me.'** The distinction between discrimination and judgment is a fine line heavily laced with the observer's own degree of soul evolution. *We all choose to learn our lessons,* **Balance** *our karma, and release stuck energy in our* <u>own</u> *time (when the* <u>soul</u> *is ready) and in a manner necessary for our* <u>own</u> *soul evolution.*

Nonetheless, there *is* some value in speaking of 'better' energy versus 'worse' energy, or 'high<u>er</u> vibration' versus 'low<u>er</u> vibration.' Notice that these are *relative* terms which imply a qualitative distinction *without necessarily any judgment* regarding 'good' versus 'bad.' For example, it makes sense to say that orange is more red than green or that orange is less green than yellow. Neither of those statements imply anything regarding the relative 'goodness' of those four colors. They are simply more or less different from each other in qualitative ways—even though they are ultimately quantifiable. Similarly, some sounds are lower while other sounds are higher. We couldn't have music at all if there weren't different tones!

Now consider the following examples: Most people are likely to describe anger as 'better' than revenge. However, most people are also likely to consider both of these states as 'bad' or 'negative.' Similarly, most people would likely say that both optimism and hopefulness are 'good' or 'positive.' They would also probably say that hopefulness is slightly 'worse' or 'more negative' than optimism. But not everyone would totally agree with all or even some of these assessments. When one tries to attach words to emotions, varying degrees of uncertainty and error creep in. Different words have the same (or similar) meaning, and the same word can have different meanings depending on many factors. Given this inherent uncertainty, how can one accurately assign or measure the physical vibrational frequency of any emotion? Ultimately words are just words. *It is the quality of the emotional vibration—not the words—that really matters*. Because this point has such important practical utility, I will have much more to say about it later.[B1, C6]

To reiterate, as you read through the remainder of the *Dancing with the Energy* books, keep in mind that energy is neither 'good' nor 'bad.' Some energies may be more conducive or 'better' for soul evolution than others, but that is strictly a matter of *what each individual has chosen to experience* in this lifetime (primarily as a result of lessons, karma, and stuck energy) and *how they have chosen to respond* to those experiences. *All is well. All is exactly as it should be. Energy just IS.* As William Shakespeare (1564–1616; dramatist and poet) once wrote:

- "There is nothing either good or bad, but **thinking** makes it so." ~ (*Hamlet*, Act II, Scene 2)

So, what is the key to 'raising your vibration' in the spiritual sense? It is not the physicist's or musician's definition of frequency at all. Science cannot measure it and, musically, it makes no sense. Nor does it have anything to do with good, bad, or any other judgmental term. Any and all comparisons (judgments) are like apples and oranges; they are completely different. Rather, it has everything to do with the degree of *Alignment* with your Higher Self in thought, word, and deed, every moment of your life. It is unique to you, and it is a qualitative dimension.

General Principles of Dancing with the Energy

There are three major *Principles of Energy* I will discuss in greater detail as they are applicable to every chapter of the three *Dancing with the Energy* books. These General Principles of Energy are the basis of soul evolution as well as successfully navigating life on the earth plane in all its manifestations. Understanding these principles and consistently using them to your advantage in everyday life (*Conscious Living*) will greatly enhance your ability to become the Master of your life.

#1 Align/Harmonize with Higher-Self Energy

By far the most important Energy Principle is that of *Alignment*, or *Harmony*, specifically, aligning/harmonizing your life, moment-to-moment, with the energy of your Higher Self. This is the fundamental basis not only of soul evolution, but of manifesting, healing, satisfying relationships, or performing any task to your peak potential. All of these will occur much more quickly, more successfully, and with far less discomfort when they become purposeful, *conscious* activities. I will have much more to say about this later.[B3, C5]

Chapter 2: It's All About the Energy!

But most people *unconsciously **Align*** their lives to the energy of the lower Self through habit, conditioning, fear, and doubt. Even when you are consciously trying your best to do everything you can to raise your vibration, the lower Self creeps in and you are all too soon unwittingly under its control. Awareness of the Higher Self and good intentions are simply not sufficient to counteract the tricks and tactics of the Self. They are habitual, reinforced over many lifetimes, and, as I've said to my students countless times, "Old habits die hard."

How can you tell when you have been seduced by the Self? The answer to this question is simple: Moment-to-moment, ask yourself, "How do I feel right now?" "Is what I have been doing making me feel better or worse?" "Is what I am about to do going to make me feel better or worse?"

If the answer to these questions is "Good" or "Better," you are in the process of ***Aligning*** yourself with the Higher Self, with Source, God, Ultimate Being, or whatever you choose to call that energy. If the answer is "Bad" or "Worse," you are aligning yourself with the energy of the Lower Self rather than your Higher Self.

Now, you have a simple choice between doing what makes you feel good/better or doing what makes you feel bad/worse. It is really quite simple—providing you remember to do it! Simple, yes. Easy, no. But it can be done. I wrote the *Dancing with the Energy* books to help ***you*** to do the work that ***only YOU can do.***

There are other cues you can use to diagnose your ***Alignment/Harmony*** as well. Table 2-1 contrasts the kinds of ***feelings*** you will have when you are in *Alignment* with the Higher Self and when you are in alignment with the Self.

23

Table 2-1
Alignment/Harmony with Your Higher Self

Alignment/Harmony	Nonalignment/Disharmony
Feeling Better or Feeling Good	Feeling Worse or Feeling Bad
Feeling Positive	Feeling Negative
Feeling Expansive	Feeling Contractive
Feeling Allowance	Feeling Resistance
It Feels "Right"	It Feels "Wrong"

Your feelings will always tell you the direction to go even when your mind (thoughts) are conflicted, confused, or even just not true. But this is not yet a habit for most people. Until such time as you can successfully implement the battle strategies and tactics of Conscious Living, your life will continue to be governed primarily by the Self (fear, doubt, conditioning, etc.) rather than by Higher Self.

#2 BALANCE YOUR ENERGIES

As a reminder, ***everything has a purpose, and that purpose ultimately is soul evolution.*** If ***Alignment/Harmony*** with your Higher Self is the most important energy principle, the ***Principle of Balance*** is the most important way to achieve it. In essence, *Balancing is the process of restoring your energies to their natural state, that is, **Alignment/Harmony with Higher Self.***

You are here on the earth plane to experience life in ***all*** its manifestations and to learn to ***balance all the energies of life*** in order to raise your consciousness and become the Master of your life. The concept of ***Balance*** is crucial to everything in the *Dancing with the Energy* series, and it is something I'll be coming back to in nearly every chapter.

Chapter 2: It's All About the Energy!

What is meant by '*Balance the energies of life?*' As an unknown pundit once put it, "There's more to *balance* than not falling over." Unbalanced energy is always unstable; it is always seeking resolution to a more grounded, more fundamental state of rest (*Balance*). You may have heard the term 'Ground of Being.' This is simply another term often used in reference to Source, God, Ultimate Being, etc. It is the part of YOU that is your Higher Self as described in the previous chapter, and it is the goal or end state (***Alignment***) of ***Balancing*** your energy.

There are several aspects to ***Balancing*** the energies of life. First, you have to balance the energies left over from past lives which *always* involves one or more of the following:

- Learning unlearned lessons
- Balancing karma
- Releasing past-life energy, including the concept of "taking care of unfinished business"

Unlearned lessons[B2, C3] are a form of unbalanced energy in that ***Alignment/Harmony*** with Source can be restored *only* through the learning of life lessons. Karma[B2, C4] also involves ***Balancing*** through the *Balancing* of karmic energy. Similarly, emotional attachment to past-life or trapped energy[B2, C5] holds you back from raising your consciousness and demands resolution in the form of non-attachment, thus *Balancing* the energy. Why are ***Balancing*** the energies of lessons, karma, and past-life energy so important? Because they ***Allow*** you to achieve greater ***Alignment*** with Source energy, facilitate soul evolution, and better enable you to become the Master of your life.

Balance is not a matter of adding all the pluses and minuses to get zero. Rather it is a matter of *eliminating the 'negative' (lower) energy frequencies* of your body, mind, and spirit so that all that is left is 'positive' (higher), such as well-being, abundance, love, God. How can you do that? Non-attachment! Simple, yes; easy, no. For each of us, non-attachment generally takes time and a good deal of work, but it is the doorway to progress and ultimate freedom. This critically important topic is discussed in detail in several chapters in each of the *Dancing with the Energy* books.

Balancing the energies of life also involves learning to balance the energies that raise your consciousness (mentioned previously) with those of living daily life (physical and material) on the earth plane. You have to learn to deal with *all* the energies of life constructively in order to raise your consciousness and become the Master of your life. ***You have to learn to live in the world but not be of (attached to) the world in order to raise your consciousness.*** When you finally learn this simple (but difficult) lesson, you will find that *everything* in life just *flows* much more smoothly, more efficiently, and you will experience life as much happier and more joyful.

Thus, ***Balance*** is not only a major theme of this book, but I will refer to it repeatedly in terms of how to *restore balance* in the major energies of life on the earth plane. In particular, the concept of ***Dynamic Balance*** is discussed later in greater detail.[B1, C8]

Everything is good. Everything is perfect. All is as it should be for your learning. Soul Evolution is not about the comfort zone. It is about facing your fears and taking responsibility for becoming the Master of your life through learning your unlearned lessons, *balancing* your karma, and detaching from your self-limiting and self-defeating beliefs and the emotions which hold you to the past, *thus **Balancing** your soul and life energies.*

As indicated previously, it is not the *quantitative* aspect of energy, but the *quality* of the energy that is important, whether for soul evolution, manifesting, healing, satisfying relationships, or for

Chapter 2: It's All About the Energy!

any task performance. ***Aligning*** your conscious energy with that of your Source and ***Balancing*** the energy as described above is ***what you need to do***. The rest of the process is all about ***how you need to do it*** if you want your efforts to produce the results you desire.

#3 ALLOW THE ENERGY TO FLOW

You are a conduit, a conductor, for Source Energy. You are not the energy itself. Just as an oil pipeline that is broken or filled with mud can't efficiently convey oil from Point A to Point B, Source energy can't flow through your mind (conscious and/or subconscious) or through your body if you are not free and clear of obstructions. In other words, you need to remove the energetic blockages from your entire being in order for the energy of Spirit to flow freely through you.

The progressively higher stages of soul evolution are indicators of your *relative* success in removing the energy blockages that are holding you back. Your progress toward the next stage is essentially a matter of removing even more (and deeper) energy blocks. Thus, ***Allowing*** the energy of Spirit to work is an integral part of the entire process. In its essence, ***Allowing*** *is the process of **Balancing** your energies.*

There are two major impediments to the process of ***Allowing*** I should mention—Resistance and Energy Blocks. It is important to understand these obstacles and how they operate to fully comprehend how to reverse them and *Allow* your energy to flow unhindered.

RESISTANCE

The first and foremost obstacle is actually the opposite of ***Allowing***, that is, *resistance*. In fact, resistance is the primary source of blocking all efforts at ***Balance*** and ***Alignment/Harmony***. I will discuss later[B3, C2, C5] why it is vitally important

27

to *focus on what you want (Alignment) rather than on what you* don't *want* (resistance).

Resistance is so much easier to focus on than *Allowing* because most often it tends to occur subconsciously; we are generally not aware of it. Resistance is the most common form of the Self in action, and we all tend to practice resistance throughout each and every day of our life experience. The challenge—and indeed the secret to success in every department of life—is to **consciously and actively change your habitual mode of thinking by practicing Allowing** instead of resisting.

How can you tell when you are resisting *Alignment/Harmony* with Higher Self and when you are *Allowing* the energy of Source to flow freely through you? Easy! Look back at Table 2-1, Alignment/Harmony with Your Higher Self. If you are *feeling* good, positive, expansive, etc., you are *Allowing* Source Energy (through your Higher Self) to flow through you. If you are feeling bad, negative, contractive, etc., you are *resisting* your Higher Self. Determining whether you are allowing or resisting is easy. Consciously remembering to stop in the middle of whatever you are doing to check whether you are *Allowing* is more difficult. But the hardest part is actually following through and implementing techniques to assist in allowing your energies to flow naturally.

Even though your emphasis should be on *Allowing*, the topic of *Resistance* is so important that you need to be able to recognize the myriad ways that you display resistance and then know how to deal with it throughout each and every day in order to begin to turn it around.

ENERGY BLOCKS

Energy blocks are also a major obstacle compromising the free flow of your energies and are basically just another form of resistance. As an example, some energy blocks are quite literally the blockage of energy in the chakras of the body and/or the energy meridians.[B2, C6; B3, C2] For example, acupuncture is one (of many) means of restoring the natural flow of life energy in the body. In fact, all 'alternative' (versus conventional western medical) healing modalities in one way or another operate on the *same basic* **Principle of Allowing** *the energy to flow naturally.*

- "You ask me about energy blocks … Every thought … becomes reality. … If it is not used (which is usually the case), then it becomes stagnant, negative energy. This negative energy permeates the Auric [Etheric] Body and eventually (because it is not going anywhere) becomes stagnant. This then … gathers in the chakras and then starts to affect the physical body. You have stopped it by not acting and ***allowing*** the created energy to flow. It then turns inwards trying to get back to its creator. … That is how blockages are created. … Removing this stagnant, negative energy then ***allows*** the spiritual body to vibrate at a higher rate of vibration." ~ Maitreya (Newsletter #275, January 1, 2010)

But there are other, even more common, energy blocks we face constantly. These blocks come in the form of *conditioning* to think and behave in certain ways influenced by our nationality, culture, family, friends, etc. They are called 'social norms' in the psychological and sociological literature, and they all have to do with regulating our thoughts (and consequently our feelings) and especially our behavior, even in situations in which other people are not involved or present. I will refer to conditioning extensively throughout the remainder of the *Dancing with the Energy* books.

The most insidious and pervasive energy blocks of all, however, are *worry, fear, and doubt*. These are the prime tools used by the Self to keep you under its control and prevent you from raising your level of consciousness. While they are often triggered by current situations in life, each of us has faced such situations hundreds, even thousands, of times in every lifetime we have ever lived. The roots of fear and doubt are deeply embedded in the soul memory and replay continuously in our lives today even though we don't realize it consciously.

Think about the number of times you have faced fear and/or doubt in your life. If you are like many of us, sometimes (or even most of the time) you ran away from the situation. How do you *feel* about those incidents in your past? Probably not so good.

Now think about the number of times in your life when you faced fear or doubt and worked your way through it. If you are like most of us, there are likely far fewer examples of facing fear than of running away from it. How do you *feel* right now about those times when you faced your fear? You probably *feel* quite good about those incidents.

Facing fears and doubts *feels* a whole lot better than running from them, doesn't it? So why do we run away? Well, that is the nature of fear, and the Self knows it all too well. Things actually start to change once you face your fear. After that, the fear diminishes or disappears entirely.

- "There is one barrier to your achieving your goal of learning and that is fear. Fear is the worst energy you can have. It will stop you dead in your tracks. It will keep you a slave to your life lessons, stopping you from moving on. ... If you have fear in your life then you have no growth, for the fear will stop you from growing. Look your fear in the face and see it for what it is, an illusion that you have created, and you will move forward and grow. It is not easy letting go of fear, but once it is faced, it becomes nothing, absolutely nothing! Why not face your fear?" ~ Maitreya (Newsletter #242, September 10, 2009)

Tips for Allowing the Energy to Flow

TIP #1 – DETACH FROM 'STUCK' ENERGY

Detach from stagnant or 'stuck' energy (for example, unlearned lessons, karma, past-life energy, lost love, disappointment, unmet expectations, unrewarded effort, negativity of any kind). This is the single most effective thing you can do to battle resistance and restore the natural flow of energy, thereby *Allowing* the energy of Higher Self to flow naturally in your life. *Non-attachment* does not come easily for most of us, but it can be learned and practiced. It is such an important topic that I will discuss it in considerable detail in several chapters of each book in the *Dancing with the Energy* series.

TIP #2 – FEEL—DON'T JUST THINK

Not that thinking is bad, but the Self *loves* it when we try to think our way through or out of negativity. This automatically puts us out of **Balance**. The human brain is a master of rationalizing our experiences to 'make sense' of what is happening both around us and to us with 'logical' reasons for why, how, and who is responsible.[B1, C6] As of the date of this writing, two Nobel Prizes support the scientific documentation of this phenomenon (Herbert Simon, Economics, 1978; [(1916–2001; political scientist, economist, sociologist, psychologist, and computer scientist], and Daniel Kahneman, Economics, 2002 [1934–;cognitive psychologist in judgment and decision-making]).

Sounds a lot like the Self, doesn't it? That's because the Self has complete access to your soul history embedded in the subconscious mind. It knows all the tricks to play and it knows all the 'emotional buttons' to push in order to gain and maintain control of your conscious, 'rational' mind. Remember, soul evolution, manifesting, healing, satisfying relationships, or performing any task to your peak potential is far more about learning to use your *intuition* than it is about following any rational (and especially self-deluding!) logic.

TIP #3 – GO WITH THE FLOW

You have probably heard the phrase, *"Go with the flow."* What does that mean, exactly? To some people it means that destiny or fate is in charge and that there is no use in fighting it. Just go along with whatever happens because it is inevitable. To others, 'Go with the flow' means simply to go along with the crowd, do what is expected or what is socially acceptable in a given situation (conditioning). It is much easier than 'bucking the tide,' standing up for what <u>*you*</u> *want to think or do* rather than what others think or what they want you to do. Doesn't sound much like becoming your own Master, does it? I'll address the question of destiny later[B2, C2] but, for the moment, let's consider what it means metaphysically to 'Go with the flow.'

Remember, I am talking about **Allowing** the energy to *flow* here. That energy is who-you-really-are, your Higher Self. Not going with the flow of your Higher Self is called **resistance**, which was mentioned in Table 2-1 under the heading of **Alignment/Harmony**. No matter what it is labeled, resistance **never** *feels* right; it doesn't *feel* good. It occurs when you know there is something you should do but you don't want to do it. It happens because the Self is pushing back on your efforts to raise

Chapter 2: It's All About the Energy!

your vibration, and it is often quite a battle, much like what goes on in the Dark Night of the Soul of Cosmic Consciousness.[B1, C1]

The higher meaning of the phrase, '*Go with the flow*' is simply to *watch for emotional resistance, stop, and **Allow*** yourself to *go with the flow of Higher Self energy* in order to ***Balance*** and ***re-Align*** with Higher Self. You can easily tell whether you are in resistance or *Allowance* by *how you feel* as discussed previously.

To go with the flow also means *not to push for doing something your way or on your time schedule*. That is the Self subtly (or not-so-subtly) using your ***ego*** to push against (resist) the *real you*, your Higher Self. And not just against your Higher Self. When you argue for or insist on doing things *your way*, you tend to get 'push-back' (resistance) from other people. Only when you stop *pushing* and start ***Allowing*** will you begin to really make progress toward your goals and desires.

Tip #4 – Get Out of the Way!

And while I'm on the topic of ego, another aspect of ***Allowing*** the energy to flow is to stand back and ***get yourself*** (literally your *Self*) ***out of the way!*** Don't muck it up with your ego! The Universe is in charge, so you don't need to get in the way. *Allow* the Universe to provide what you need for your development—it knows better than you!

Tip #5 – Be Open

How do you get your ego out of the way? *Be open to possibilities, opportunities, and new experiences* (physical, mental, and spiritual). All of these imply *being open to and embracing change*. The Self hates change and tries to keep you in the comfort zone in order to maintain control. Embracing rather than resisting change ***Allows*** you to raise your vibration more quickly and greatly facilitates your soul evolution. I'll discuss the topic of change in much greater detail later.[B3, C6]

Summary of General Energy Principles

These three Energy Principles—***Alignment/Harmony, Balance***, and ***Allowing*** the energy to flow—are the fundamental bases of all energy work. In the battle between the Self and the Higher Self, ***Alignment/Harmony*** is the objective, ***Balance*** is the strategy or plan for achieving that objective and ***Allowing*** is the set of methods or moment-to-moment tactics that make the battle plan operational (see Figure 2-1).

Figure 2-1
Process of Soul Evolution

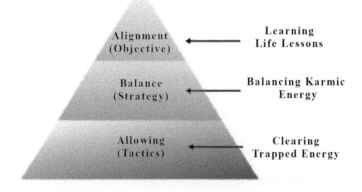

You can't fully ***Balance*** your energy without ***Allowing*** it to flow unhindered, and you can't completely ***Align*** with Higher Self without *Balancing* your energy. If you want to achieve *Alignment/Harmony*, you must begin the process with the basics—*Allowing* the energy of YOUR Higher Self to flow freely without resistance. But don't think for a moment that you have to start at the bottom and work your way up. If you do, you will almost certainly never get there!

You must *always* work toward **Alignment** *first* if you really want to make progress. To be sure, **resisting** or **not allowing** will certainly derail **Balancing** your energy and, hence, *Alignment* as well. But if you don't keep aiming at the bull's-eye, you can shoot arrows of effort all day (life) long and never even come close to hitting the target! It is important to *work toward all three levels simultaneously.* **Allowing is critical, Balancing is essential, but the objective—Alignment—is paramount.**

Thoughts are Energy!

It is axiomatic that *doing anything consciously requires some degree of thought.* It is often said in metaphysical circles that "Energy follows thought." In other words, thought gives rise to energy or, alternatively, ***thought is energy.***

Maitreya expresses this concept repeatedly. As just one example:

- "All thought is energy, and all energy has to move forward.... Energy as thought has only one purpose and that is to create what has been thought. Negative thoughts will create negative realities; positive thoughts will create positive realities." ~ Maitreya (Newsletter #275, January 1, 2010)

Even if you are engaged in some 'mindless' activity, you are still thinking, just not consciously using your thoughts to your best advantage. ***Thought is energy***, and it is so important that I devote an entire chapter to it later in this book.[B1, C5]

Emotions are Energy!

An important concept in this series of books is that of *taking action vibrationally—through your feelings*. Your emotions—your feelings—are a major key not only to your daily experience of life, but also to *Alignment*, *Balance*, and *Allowing* the energy to flow. I will cover the topic of emotions in much greater detail in Chapter 6 of this book as well as in Books 2 and 3 in the chapters discussing how they are involved in past-life energy, healing, manifesting, etc. For now, consider just the following:

- "All emotion is energy. Just imagine that. Then imagine not releasing that energy but keeping it within you to fester and bubble away like a boil or a big sore on your body. I can see some of you expressing disgust at this statement, but this is what happens when you do not express your feelings, do not speak your truth quietly and clearly, and do not deal with past-life energy. All unused energy stays within the physical body and in the soul memory. If it is not expressed, it becomes a problem not only in this life, but often in many incarnations to come. The energy has not been cleared and so it stays there waiting for the opportunity in a future incarnation to do so. You can ask of me, 'But Maitreya, why do you allow this, why does the Ultimate Being allow this?' But we do not allow it; it is you, with your fear, doubt and insecurity, that creates this situation—nobody else." ~ Maitreya (Newsletter #164, September 26, 2005)

The Soul Itself is Energy!

The Soul itself is energy, an aspect, a spark, a piece, a component, an extension—whatever term feels comfortable to you—of that Divine Energy known as Source, Ultimate Being, God, or whatever term for that energy that best resonates with you. In essence, *your soul is God expressing or manifesting as YOU*. This concept was expressed in the *Vedas* of ancient India (c. 1500 – c. 500 BCE). Maitreya simply says:

- "Whether you know God as the Creator, Mother/Father God, Divine Soul, this energy is with you, all around you, and all embracing."~ Maitreya (Newsletter #309, April 9, 2010)

Summary of Energy Principles and Tips for Allowing

GENERAL PRINCIPLES OF ENERGY

- #1 Align/Harmonize with Higher-Self Energy
- #2 Balance Your Energy
- #3 Allow the Energy to Flow

TIPS FOR ALLOWING THE ENERGY TO FLOW

- Tip #1 – Detach from 'Stuck' Energy
- Tip #2 – FEEL—Don't <u>Just</u> Think
- Tip #3 – Go with the Flow
- Tip #4 – Get Out of the Way!
- Tip #5 – Be Open

Conscious Living and Energy

*"It's **All** About the Energy!"* The key to successful living in any realm—material, physical, emotional, or spiritual—is *learning how to use that energy* to your best advantage to become the Master of *your* life and to create the life *you* desire. That is the practice of **Conscious Living** which is discussed throughout this book and in greater detail later.[B1, C8; B2, C1]

Chapter 3: Human Energy Fields and the Ancient Wisdoms

Introduction

In the *Yoga Sutras*, Patanjali (circa 5th to 2nd century BCE; philosopher, author, and compiler of the *Yoga Sutras*) refers to four *subtle bodies* or *subtle energy fields*—which give rise to and animate the physical body. Some authors occasionally refer to these four subtle bodies as 'bio-energetic fields.'

Let's begin by describing these subtle energy fields, what they are like, and how they function. To do that, I'll use an analogy (see Table 3-1). Think about water, plain old H_2O, in its various physical states (Column 3) from ice to liquid water, to suspended

Table 3-1
Analogy of Human Subtle Bodies to Water Molecule Density

Subtle Energy Field	Relative Density and Energy	Physical State of Water
Physical Body	5 (Highest Density, Lowest Energy)	Ice
Etheric Field or 'Etheric Body'	4	Liquid water
Emotional Field or 'Emotional Body'	3	Suspended droplets (example, mist/fog/clouds)
Mental Field or 'Mental Body'	2	Invisible gas/water vapor in humid air (example, seashore)
Spiritual Field or 'Spiritual Body'	1 (Lowest Density, Highest Energy)	Invisible gas/water vapor in relatively dry air (example, desert)

droplets (as in mist, fog, or clouds), to invisible—but humid—air (vapor), and finally to relatively dry air. In each of these physical states, the density of water molecules decreases from visible, hard ice to invisible, relatively infrequent molecules of H_2O. Regardless of its density, it is still water, H_2O.

Now think of the human subtle energy fields (Column 1) in terms of the analogy of water in its different states of molecular density (Column 2) from ice (most dense) to a gas (least dense). Like H_2O, the different 'states' of the human subtle energy fields are basically the same, just expressed at different densities or energy potentials along a continuum from high density/lower energy to low density/higher energy. Just as 'water is water' (regardless of its density), so too your subtle energy fields are all fundamentally the same (think, *'the energies of life'),* just expressed at different densities or different energy levels.

The lower the density, the higher the energy state, and the more that state interpenetrates higher density energy fields. For example, ice cannot penetrate or intermingle (combine) with an invisible gas, but long ago, scientists showed us that gases can definitely interpenetrate or intermingle with ice. Similarly, the lower density energy fields contain or interpenetrate the higher density fields because their energy is higher, but not the other way around. Think of Russian matryoshka, or nesting dolls, each one inside the next larger doll. The larger dolls contain (or 'interpenetrate') the smaller dolls. I'll speak more about this 'interpenetration' concept in the following descriptions.

The Subtle Bodies

First, the **Spiritual Energy Field**, or **Spiritual Body** as Patanjali calls it, is a part of the collective energy of Spirit often referred to as "the collective unconscious beyond individual consciousness." It is the most rarified or least dense level of energy that is part of each individual, and consequently the most powerful. It is your individual part of and direct connection with what is often called 'Source Energy' or 'The Ultimate Being' or simply 'God.' When you communicate with your Higher Self, which is your direct link to God, the Spiritual Energy Field or Spiritual Body is that with which you are in communication.

Depending on an individual's level of soul evolution (level of consciousness), the Spiritual Energy Field may extend anywhere from a few feet around the physical body, fill an entire room, fill a gymnasium, or extend even beyond the limits of human perception. As the least dense (that is, the highest energy state) of the four subtle bodies, the Spiritual Energy Field subsumes (includes, interpenetrates) all of the other subtle bodies and, consequently, the physical body as well.

Through the **Spiritual Energy Field** or **Spiritual Body**, you can connect with individual souls, typically those with whom you have had very strong relationships in this life or in past lives (for example, family members). But a 'strong relationship' can also include souls you have never known personally but with whom you identify strongly (for example, an admired teacher such as Gautama Buddha, Jesus, Maitreya, etc.).

The **Mental Energy Field** or **Mental Body** contains your individualized 'thought energies' (*patterns of disturbances or perturbations in the energy field*) from every lifetime you have ever lived, including the *memory* of the emotions you felt at the time.

The Mental Energy Field extends several feet around the physical body but may be large enough to fill a large room depending on an individual's degree of concentration (intensity of thinking). This energy field contains or subsumes the other two energy bodies that are more dense. This means that one's negative thoughts and beliefs are active in blocking everything down to and including the physical body.

While there are positive and uplifting thoughts in most lifetimes, if the Mental Energy Field is full of negative and repetitive thoughts, energy blockages can quickly develop and even carry over from one lifetime to the next, remaining in the soul memory until those blockages are cleared. The Self uses these soul memories as an extremely effective tool to capitalize on negative thoughts, enhancing them or even 'creating' thoughts and emotions of fear, doubt, low self-esteem, low self-worth, etc., thereby preventing you from raising your consciousness and becoming the Master your life. Such thoughts often reinforce or even create corresponding emotions that further act to block soul evolution.

Souls with whom you are connected karmically—either as recipient or as provider—can have a profound influence on your life. In these cases, you are not dealing with the "collective unconscious beyond individual consciousness," you are dealing with the consciousness of individual souls through the Mental (and lower) Energy Fields.

The **Emotional Field** or **Emotional Body** is sometimes referred to as the Astral Field/Body and is the next most dense of the human energy fields. It contains the emotions created in the current lifetime (especially from childhood), as well as past-life emotions lodged in the soul memory. Emotions are *feeling states* in the physical body that resonate with the energy of the emotional body. We speak of *feeling down* or *bad* when experiencing relatively negative emotions and *feeling up* or *good* with more positive emotional states. The emotional body extends two to three feet around the physical body and is what clairvoyants sense or 'see' as a person's aura, the colors of which reflect that person's momentary emotions or moods.

Maitreya repeatedly tells us that one of our major tasks on the earth plane is to learn to detach from the Emotional Body. He says "*Controlling the emotional body is the only way to raise the vibration*" (Newsletter #56, September 28, 2002). The reason is that relatively negative emotions are energy blocks that must be cleared if you are to make progress on the spiritual path. The Self uses such emotions—especially those having to do with fear, low self-worth and low self-esteem, criticism, anger, etc.—to keep you mired in victimhood, self-pity, worthlessness, etc. This prevents you from raising your consciousness and becoming the Master of your life.

- *"The whole purpose of your spiritual path is to let go of and move on from the emotional body.* It is the emotional body which the Self hangs on to, holding on to the fear, doubt, jealousy, anger, greed etc. Often you are not aware that this is happening to you—that the Self is hanging on to these emotions. As you face your fear and you face all of the emotional issues which are often leftover energy from other lives, the Self has less and less to hold on to, and the Higher Self can then become a greater force in your life." ~ Maitreya (Newsletter #193, December 12, 2006)

- "So many souls are bringing to the surface incredible anger and frustration caused by others' past actions and by even their own actions in their life. One cannot move forward in vibration (raise one's consciousness) without letting go of such things. They belong to the emotional body, and the purpose of your life on the Earth plane is to ***control and learn to <u>still</u> the emotional body***. It is the energy the Self lives on, hiding away until, one day when you least expect it, the anger or frustration comes to the surface and takes you by surprise." ~ Maitreya (Newsletter #199, June 24, 2007)

Since the Emotional Energy Field is denser (lower energy state) than the Mental Energy Field, negative thoughts in the Mental Energy Field can easily create corresponding or supporting negative emotions in the Emotional Energy Field, exacerbating the blockages occurring in the emotional body. But it is a two-way street. Because the Mental Body interpenetrates the

Emotional Body, negative emotions also enhance or even create negative thoughts.[B1, C6]

The **Etheric Energy Field** or **Etheric Body** (also sometimes called the 'Vital Field' or 'Physical Energy Field') is the fourth and most dense subtle body, so it has the lowest energy state of the four. The Etheric Energy Field is the blueprint for the physical body. It houses the Life Force energy and, whenever there are problems in the physical body, the cause of those problems can be traced directly back to blocked life-force energy in the Etheric Body. Thus, energetic origins of all injuries, wounds, illnesses, etc. (including those from past lives that have not been cleared) are transmitted to and operate from the Etheric Energy Field.

The Etheric Energy Field permeates the physical body and extends outward about two inches from it. It also contains the chakras (described later in this chapter). The chakras play a prominent role in Eastern medicine—especially the Indian traditions of Hinduism and Buddhism. The Etheric Energy Field also contains the energy meridians used in Chinese acupuncture and related healing modalities that I will cover later.[B3, C2]

Figure 3-1 illustrates Patanjali's subtle bodies and their relationship to each other. Because the Etheric Field (darkest shade) is the most sense subtle energy field, it is contained within the Emotional Body (lighter shade), Mental Body (still lighter shade), and the Spiritual Body (lightest shade) similar to Russian matryoshka, or nesting dolls. Consequently, as the blueprint for the physical body, negative thoughts and emotions have an enormous impact on the healthy functioning of the Etheric Energy Field as well as the physical body.

**Figure 3-1
Patanjali's Subtle Bodies**

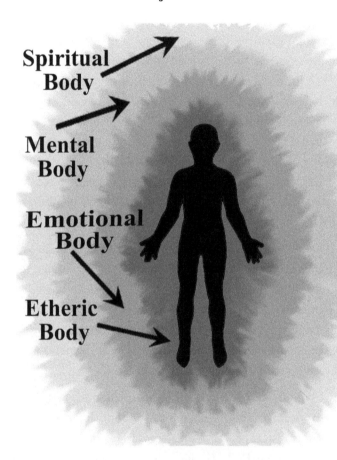

Comments on the Subtle Bodies

ARE THERE REALLY FOUR SUBTLE BODIES?

The subtle energy fields of which our souls and physical bodies are made are not distinct and separate, but are a *continuum*

Chapter 3: Human Energy Fields and the Ancient Wisdoms

of the same energy. However, this energy is expressed at different densities (energy potentials), much like ice, liquid water, visible droplets suspended in the air (such as fog, clouds), and invisible water vapor (humidity) are all different energy states of the same substance, water (see Table 3-1).

Another example is a glass of water in which you stir in a spoonful of dirt. After you let it sit for an hour or so, notice that the bottom of the glass is filled with a very fluid mud, a thin mixture of water and dirt. Above the mud, the water is extremely cloudy, a little less cloudy halfway up the glass, and almost clear at the top of the glass. The glass is filled with water and dirt, but it is separated into 'layers' from the highest density at the bottom to lowest density at the top, and the boundary between layers is almost indistinguishable. The glass contains a continuous column of water and dirt that has different densities (thicknesses or concentrations) from top to bottom.

The purpose of talking about different subtle energy fields is to be able to communicate ideas more simply and with some structure. When the Indian teacher Patanjali wrote about these ideas in the 5th–2nd century BCE, the bulk of his audience had little formal education and was not used to thinking in terms of a 'continuum' varying along some 'dimension.' Most people in India back then had never seen ice, let alone have a word in their language for it. Nor did they understand that ice and water vapor (if they even had the concepts of ice or vapor) are essentially the same thing. Patanjali was simply trying to describe a 'truth' as he understood it in terms that other people of his time and culture could understand.

Whether there are three, four, seven, or however many subtle energy fields (there are authoritative sources for all of these) is really of little consequence. It is all the same energy, just qualitatively a little different in each different explanation. What is important is whether the distinctions along any continuum are meaningful to the people who communicate using any particular system. An analogy here is some people communicating differences in temperature in degrees Celsius vs. degrees Fahrenheit, or distance in kilometers vs. miles. If I were asked how much gasoline (or is it petrol?) my car's tank holds, I could give you one number in liters, but an entirely different number in gallons. And then there is the US gallon versus the Imperial gallon. The point is that the concepts are the same but the language used is different and often culturally determined.

Whether there are exactly three subtle energy fields or four or seven, or whatever, only makes a difference if one number better helps to communicate the underlying idea. *Use whatever works for you.* For purposes of our discussion in this book, however, Patanjali's four subtle energy fields help to communicate the following:

- The *Spiritual Energy Field or Body* recognizes that all human consciousness comes from one Source and that every human consciousness (or soul) is part of a whole (the collective unconscious beyond individual consciousness) along with every other soul (individualized consciousness).

- The *Mental Energy Field or Body* recognizes that individual consciousness is characterized by thoughts, that your thoughts are the essence of your individual identity, and that through your thoughts you are the creator of your own individual reality.

- The *Emotional Energy Field or Body* (also sometimes called the 'Astral Body') is characterized by individual feeling states or emotions. Our emotions add an evaluative dimension (good versus bad) to our thoughts, and thus have an incredible influence on how human beings *interpret* 'reality.'

- The ***Etheric Energy Field or Body*** (sometimes called the 'Physical Energy Field') is the 'blueprint' ('immediate energetic cause,' 'immediate energetic sculptor') of any given physical body with all its unique characteristics. This applies especially to characteristics that cannot otherwise be explained by the modern science of genetics, which was unknown for another 2500 + years after Patanjali's time!

If these four subtle energy fields help you to understand the energies of life, great! If not, then use some other system that better speaks to your truth and that helps you to communicate something meaningful to others, for example, the perspective of modern quantum physics.[B1, C4]

SOUL MEMORIES

Soul memories are actually carried in the ***Spiritual Energy Field or Body*** (the Matrix[B1, C4]) but can interact with any or all of the other subtle bodies in various ways. For example:

- A karmic injury in a previous life may manifest through the subtle bodies into the physical body in this life as an injury, a congenital condition, or even as a birth defect.

- Soul memories of having been wronged or abandoned may attach to the mental field, as thoughts of anger, especially if there are also thoughts of guilt about betraying or abandoning someone in another past life.

- Soul memories of loneliness or unhappiness at the tragic death of people we once knew may attach to the emotional field as sadness or grief.

- Memories of dead children from a past life may attach to the uterine area of the etheric field and, consequently the body, creating infertility issues, problems with delivery, or even the fear of having children.

Any or all of these kinds of soul memories can create mental, emotional, etheric, and/or physical blocks which, if not cleared or released will, at a minimum, stop your progression on the spiritual path. At some point they will likely manifest in the physical body as injury, illness or disease, and/or psychological stress (dis-ease).

ENERGY BLOCKS

Unexpressed thoughts, unresolved feelings and emotions, and words are all energies. All these energies are imprinted as 'images' or 'memories' in the subtle bodies from past lives and from the current life. They are called 'unused' energy, 'trapped' energy, or blockages. Later in *Dancing with the Energy*, I will briefly identify several therapies and healing techniques that can bring these emotionally charged energies to the surface for release and healing or transformation so that they no longer have the power to control your life.[B2, C5]

ENERGY FIELDS

How is all of this energy 'stored' in the subtle bodies? (The term 'resonate' might be a better word to use.) Remember, ***It's All About the Energy!*** Your unexpressed thoughts, unresolved feelings and emotions, your actions and your words are all energies that you created at some point either in this lifetime or in a previous life. They are a part of the 'individualized you'—part of the collection of energies called the soul. Those energies all have their own density and, by *Law of Attraction*, they 'resonate with' or are attracted to similar energies.

- The energies of past physical bodies—their strengths and weaknesses—gather together by *Law of Attraction* to form the **Etheric Energy Field** and are added to by the physical condition of your body during the present life.

- Your individualized past-life emotions aggregate by *Law of Attraction* and are called the **Emotional Energy Field** or **Emotional Body**. These emotions are then added to and are modified by your current life experiences.

- The energies of your old individual thoughts coalesce by *Law of Attraction* (including those from this lifetime), and that collection of energies is called the **Mental Body** or the **Mental Energy Field**.

- The **Spiritual Energy Field** is where all souls, indeed all the energy and matter of creation, are 'connected' in the singular 'energy' of Source, God, All-That-Is, etc.

Together the *subtle bodies* or *energy fields* are a continuous, indestructible energy field from high density to low density that makes up what is called the '*soul memory*.' But it is all just the qualitatively different energies on a continuum of density that is the soul, the 'me,' all contained in or subsumed by the **Spiritual Energy Field** or **Spiritual Body**.

Energy cannot be destroyed; it can only be transformed. Soul evolution ('raising your vibration,' 'raising your consciousness') is a matter of ***transforming*** the energy that is the individualized essence of 'you,' your soul. Sometimes this is done through 'learning your lessons,' and sometimes through 'healing,' which basically involves transforming dysfunctional energies into more positive, more functional life energies.

If you have amplified these past-life energies with the energy of 'attachment'—that is, you 'hold on' to these energies and don't *Allow* them to flow freely—they fester like an infection in the subtle energy fields. Eventually they will manifest in the physical body as pain, disease, emotional problems, and/or psychological dis-ease (for example, stress, mental problems, etc.).

Controlling the Energy Fields

Why is it important to *control* the subtle bodies or energy fields, and how is it done? Maitreya answers the first part of this question very succinctly:

- "There are many spiritual people today, who have beautiful spiritual gifts and are wonderful healers or light workers for us in the Spirit world, but they still have not controlled one or more of their subtle bodies. Until they do this they cannot move forward to a higher level." ~ Maitreya (Newsletter #244, September 23, 2009)

"Controlling the subtle bodies" is simply Maitreya's way of talking about controlling the Self in order to bring about *Balance* and ultimately, *Aligning/Harmonizing* your life energies with the Higher Self. This is absolutely necessary if you want to raise your level of consciousness and become the Master of your life.

Controlling the subtle bodies begins with controlling the physical body in terms of *excessive or compulsive desires* (for example, food, sex, stimulants, etc.). This is because what happens in your physical body over time modifies or changes the energy in the subtle bodies. Note that Maitreya is *not advocating some form of asceticism or denial, but moderation (Balance)*. He is speaking of *Conscious Living* as a means of enhancing soul evolution. Once you have attained a higher stage of conscious awareness, the ***desire*** for possessions, destructive habits and behaviors—even addictions—that hold you back from raising your consciousness will become less and less until they fall away naturally of their own accord. ***Soul evolution cannot be forced, but you can encourage and accelerate it through Conscious Living.***

Maitreya says that "Each subtle body has a Self and a Higher Self, and one must attain the Higher Self in *everything*." (Newsletter #244, September 23, 2009)

For example: The etheric body is brought under control through practices that contribute to good physical and mental health as described above. But Maitreya repeatedly tells us that our primary goal on the earth plane is to learn to detach from the emotional body. Why? Because it is the primary tool used by the (lower) Self to maintain control and to stop us dead in our tracks on the path of soul evolution. In the mental body, we have to learn to control all of our thoughts. Remember, it is thought that creates, and negative thoughts about anything prevent us from raising our vibration higher. Finally, Maitreya admonishes us to control the spiritual body by learning to use it wisely. This is done through developing and trusting our intuitive (psychic) capabilities and understanding that the universal energy is for the benefit of all, not just for our own selfish desires.

Maitreya concludes his explanation as follows:

- "The path to controlling the Selves in each subtle body is a long and arduous task. It will not happen overnight and at the least will take ten to fifteen years of earth time from when you start your path of learning. All kinds of tests are thrown in your way. The purpose of all incarnations is to free you of the limitations you have placed in your subtle

bodies. However, when you return to the earth plane for another incarnation, the Self takes control again and the battle between the Self and the Higher Self begins. Many incarnations go by before the control of the subtle bodies is achieved. Sometimes souls plead for help in freeing themselves of their limitations and ask ... for assistance. A teacher or a healer is then found to help them, and arrangements made to work with them in an incarnation."
~ Maitreya (Newsletter #244, September 23, 2009)

REMOVING ENERGY BLOCKS

There are several ways either to release or to transform energy blocks from the subtle bodies. These will be discussed in greater detail in subsequent chapters.[B2, C5; B3, C2] Thoughts from the Mental Energy Field, emotions from the Emotional Energy Field, and past-life physical conditions (for example, old wounds, diseases, disabilities, psychological traumas) in the Etheric Energy Field are brought into one's conscious awareness as memories of people, places, events, emotions, and physical maladies, as well as their unique 'energy signatures.' These energy signatures are how you recognize souls, places, and events as familiar or even identifiable even though you have never encountered them in this life. For example, you might recognize your mother in a past life as your Uncle Bob in this life. Various procedures are then used to unblock the trapped or stagnant energies that have come into your awareness.

The Chakras

The concept of chakras comes from ancient Hinduism and Buddhism and derives from the Sanskrit word for 'wheel' or 'turning,' referring to the manner in which energy seems to radiate out from them in an alternating, spinning fashion. Another translation from the yogic context is 'vortex' or 'whirlpool,' again with the spinning connotation. In essence, the chakras can be thought of as 'energy pumping stations.'

Chakras are subtle, or energetic, centers of energy within the physical body, and are located along the etheric spine (the Sushumna, which runs up and down the central axis of the body within the physical spine between the crown (top of the head) and sacrum (tailbone). The chakras have a number of 'spokes' or 'petals' radiating out from their center, and their *state of **Balance*** is reflected in your physical and mental health.

Specific chakras supply the etheric energy to specific major body organs and glands to which they are energetically linked by vibrational similarity. The chakras, themselves, are similarly governed by the four subtle energy fields just discussed.

Much like the question regarding the precise number of subtle bodies, the number of chakras depends on your purpose and the message you want to communicate. There are a number of different chakra systems in use, each with a long and successful tradition behind it. For example, Pranic Healing uses 13 major chakras, and occasionally a number of minor chakras. In fact, every joint in the body—over 300 in all—is considered a 'mini-chakra.' Generally speaking, however, even Pranic Healing rarely uses more than 13 major chakras.

Traditionally, there are seven chakras referred to in spiritual development. I once asked Maitreya, my teacher in Spirit, whether there are more than seven chakras, and he basically gave me the same answer as I just gave you. He said, "Yes, there are more than seven chakras, but few people are able to make use of more than seven, so for now keep it simple; just keep it at seven chakras."

The question is, "What works best for the purpose at hand?" My purpose in the *Dancing with the Energy* books is education about **Conscious Living** and the practical daily usage of the energies of life, not the 'nitty gritty' details of a specific healing modality, so I will focus on the traditional (seven) main chakras with which most people are familiar.

The ***1st Chakr***a is called the ***Root or Base Chakra*** and is located at the base of the spine. It is the foundation of the physical body. Its primary function is to provide:

- energy to the physical body
- vitality
- grounding
- physical strength
- survival
- sexuality

The ***2nd Chakra*** is called the ***Navel or Sacral Chakra***. It is located at the lower abdomen about 2 inches below the navel and provides an overload capacity for too much negative energy in the base chakra. The primary function of the 2nd Chakra is to focus energy for:

- creativity
- reproduction
- manifesting and prosperity
- value and self-worth

The ***3rd Chakra*** is called the ***Solar Plexus Chakra*** and is located midway between the lower end of the breastbone and the navel. It is the center of Self, personal power, and emotions in the human body. The primary function of the 3rd Chakra is to focus energy for:

- safety
- security
- joy
- fun
- happiness
- intellect

The **4th Chakra** is called the **Heart Chakra**. It is located at the center of the chest and is the vibrational center of love and emotions. The heart is the 'seat of the soul' in the physical body. Your true connection to Higher Self is through the heart. When your heart chakra is closed, you cut off your connection to your Higher Self, to your soul. You feel lost and abandoned. When you listen to your heart, you listen to your Higher Self. The primary function of the 4th Chakra is to focus energy for:

- loving oneself and others
- compassion
- unconditional love

The **5th Chakra** is the **Throat Chakra**. Its primary function is to focus energy for:

- communication in general
- speaking your truth
- creative expression on the mental level
- your thoughts and how you think

The **6th Chakra** is called the **Third-Eye Chakra** and is located at the forehead just above the eyes between the eyebrows. It is the center of psychic power (also called the "sixth sense"). Its primary function is to focus energy for:

- intuition
- psychic abilities such as clairvoyance, clairaudience, clairsentience, inspiration, and spiritual connection

The **7th Chakra** is called the **Crown Chakra** and is located at the top of head. It is the center of the connection to the Universe and to the spiritual side of life. Many religions call this universal energy God, Ultimate Being, Qi, or Source Energy. The primary function of the 7th Chakra is to focus energy for:

- opening to creativity
- activating intuition
- increasing psychic awareness
- connecting to higher consciousness

Before examining the relationships between the chakras and the subtle energy fields remember that there is no clear separation between the subtle bodies. They are on a continuum from least dense (the spiritual energy field) to most dense (the etheric energy field). But there are no clear lines of separation between them—they blend together with less dense layers interpenetrating more dense layers.

As I point out the connections between the subtle bodies and the chakras in the following discussion, keep in mind that the same principle applies. The 'connections' or 'links' are really describing greater degrees of vibrational similarity based on the universal *Law of Attraction*. I will use the 'connection' and 'link' terminology, however, because of long historical usage and because it is usually easier for most people to conceptualize these relationships in that fashion.

Figure 3-2 illustrates the physical body, the subtle energy fields, and the chakras. The chakras are energy centers within the physical body and are arranged directly in front of the Sushumna, the Sanskrit term for the etheric spine. The prana, Sanskrit for "life-force energy" ("chi" in Chinese and "ki" in Japanese philosophy and medicine) flows up through the Irda and down through the

Pingala, energy channels on either side of the Sushumna. As long as the prana (chi, ki, etc.) flows freely (***Allowing***), the body and its human occupant are healthy and happy (in ***Balance***). However, abnormal energy flows (either too much or too little are forms of *resistance*) in one or more chakras creates imbalance in the system with physical, emotional, mental, and spiritual health consequences (which are beyond the scope of our purpose in this book).

Figure 3-2
The Subtle Bodies & Chakras

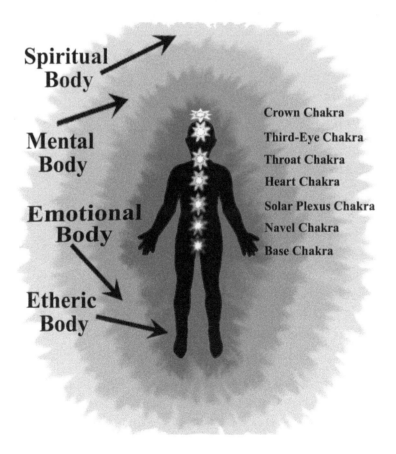

Although the chakras are energy fields within the physical body, healing practitioners sometimes treat them as unrelated to Patanjali's subtle bodies even though he, himself, was quite specific about these relationships (see Table 3-2).

Table 3-2
Direct Relationships Between
the Subtle Energy Fields and the Chakras

Chakra	Spiritual Body	Mental Body	Emotional Body	Etheric Body
Crown	X			
Third-Eye		X		
Throat		X		
Heart	X	X	X	X
Solar Plexus			X	X
Navel			X	X
Base			X	X

Note that the Spiritual Body (energy field) is *directly* connected to both the Crown and Heart chakras, illustrating why the heart energy is so important to spiritual development. The Mental Body is *directly* linked to the Third-Eye, Throat, and Heart Chakras. Both the Emotional Body and the Etheric Body are *directly* linked to the Heart, Solar Plexus, Navel, and Base chakras. The relationships with these latter bodies emphasize the close connection between one's emotions and physical health.

The Heart chakra is the only chakra *directly* connected to all four energy fields or subtle bodies. Think of it as the '***Balance point***' of the chakra system, hence its relative importance for all of life's energies.

Also note that a given emotion can lodge in more than one chakra because the energies of adjacent chakras are not completely separated; they overlap. As energy centers, they vibrate at different relative frequencies, but their respective energies are also on a continuum, so the outer energetic 'edge' of one chakra can blend into the outer energetic 'edge' of an adjacent chakra. Thus, an emotion whose vibratory frequency is close to the frequency of the 'mixing zone' between chakras can be associated with or linked to both chakras. You just have to get used to thinking of any and all energies as actually falling on a continuum rather than being carved up into separate chunks. The chunks or categories are sometimes easier to think about and to communicate to others, but they are also inaccurate distortions of what is really going on and often can lead to confusion.

The important point is that negative subconscious emotions can interfere with the healthy functioning of *any and all* of the chakras. Which chakra is most affected depends on the relative vibrational frequency of the specific emotion in question. Emotions tend to resonate with and lodge in chakras that closely match their frequency. It's just the *Law of Attraction* at work. Like attracts like; it's as simple as that.

There are many different chakra healing modalities available that are beyond the scope of this book. However, there are also many resources available in books, online, and or through chakra teachers and practitioners.

Conscious Living and the Ancient Wisdoms

So why bother with the 'Ancient Wisdoms' when we have the modern science of quantum physics?[B1, C4] That's like asking "Why bother with Italian or French or Spanish or Chinese or any other language when we have English?" If you have ever studied a foreign language, you realized fairly quickly that, even though the translation of individual words may be identical, the intended meaning of the sentence or phrase is frequently somewhat different; often something is lost in the translation. The Ancient Wisdoms and Quantum Physics are two very different languages—different perspectives on the same phenomena of human energy—each of which can help us to gain a better understanding of the complexity of the human experience.

Moreover, these perspectives are complementary. They are not only different perspectives on life, they allow us to integrate the best of human knowledge and wisdom from both the non-material (spiritual) and the material (scientific) worlds across nearly three millennia.

More importantly, both the Ancient Wisdoms and Quantum Physics provide an enriched understanding of—and practical solutions to—the problems we struggle with in our day-to-day lives. Remember, *"It's All about the Energy,"* and that is the essence of ***Conscious Living!***

Chapter 4:
Human Energy Fields and Quantum Physics

Introduction

The field of quantum physics originated in 1900 by the 1918 Nobel Laureate, Max Planck (1858–1947; theoretical physicist). Without intending to, it gives us new insights into the Ancient Wisdoms in ways that are both profound and useful. Let's take a brief look at a few of these insights:

The Basic Precepts of Quantum Physics

ALL MATTER IS ENERGY

First, one of the fundamental precepts of many ancient schools of wisdom tells us that the world we know—the Earth plane—is but an illusion, and Maitreya speaks of this repeatedly in his writings. Albert Einstein's famous 1905 equation, $E = mc^2$, hints at this by telling us that matter is really only energy slowed way, way down. Still, until the mid-20th century, matter was generally regarded as solid. Quantum physics, on the other hand, tells us that matter is not at all solid. In fact, there is far more empty space in 'solid' objects than there is 'stuff' (matter). All matter, including our bodies, is a swarm of electromagnetic energy fields comprising various minute atomic and sub-atomic particles vibrating in the vast reaches of empty space between them, and the rate of vibration is so rapid that they appear to be—and feel like—a solid mass. It's like looking at the spaces between the blades of an electric fan when it is stopped. Turn the fan on, however, and the spinning blades appear to be a solid object. But matter ('reality') is **all** just an **illusion**; it is just energy in vibration at different frequencies.

This can be a bit disconcerting if you are not used to the idea. In essence, there is no 'matter' *per se*. In his Nobel Prize Lecture in 1933, Werner Heisenberg (1901–1976; physicist) stated that the atom "has no physical properties at all" from the perspective of quantum mechanics. Even Albert Einstein was not fond of quantum mechanics, labeling it "spooky science." But continued research (and many Nobel Prizes later) has confirmed the validity of this basic premise.

ALL ENERGY IS FUNDAMENTALLY THE SAME

Second, that 'empty space' isn't really empty at all. Quantum physics has shown that all that 'stuff' we used to think of as matter is not only energy, but also all of it is connected energetically. That is, *it is all the same underlying energy* expressing (in matter) at different frequencies and amplitudes (strength). This energetic net or web is referred to in scientific circles as the 'Unified Energy Field', the 'Matrix', or more simply as the 'Field.' The Ancient Wisdoms used various terms—Universe, Source, God, etc.—while Abraham (channeled by Esther Hicks) frequently refers to it as 'All-That-Is.'

The *Vedas* of ancient India, written nearly 3000 years ago, state that the universe was not created. Rather, the Creator *became* the universe to experience the One through the many. Nice to know that science and spirituality are basically in agreement, but at least now we can use language that isn't as emotionally (and dogmatically) laden as many of the world's religions typically use. As William Shakespeare wrote, "That which we call a rose by any other name would smell as sweet" (*Romeo and Juliet*, Act II, Scene I).

Beyond that, however, quantum physics allows even atheists to more readily accept the notion that "No man is an island" (John Donne, clergyman and poet, "Meditation XVII," 1624). ***We are indeed all made of the same stuff—and we are all connected.***

POSSIBILITY VERSUS MANIFESTATION

So, what is the nature of this all-pervasive, all-inclusive quantum energy in the Matrix? Well, the word "quantum" in physics means a discrete quantity [amount] of energy proportional in magnitude [strength] to the frequency of the radiation it represents. In other words, the higher the frequency of vibration, the stronger the energy.

Think of a single *particle* of light (a photon) for example. But wait, the Unified Energy Field—the Matrix—is just energy, not matter or particles of anything. This energy of the Matrix can be described mathematically as a ***wave function***. Think of waves like ripples on a pond when you drop a rock into it. An even better example is a radio signal—a wave—that travels in all directions simultaneously. Think of listening to music from your car radio. Someone a few—or even hundreds—of miles away in any direction is listening to that same music at the same time as you.

The Matrix is pure energy with the <u>potential</u> to manifest infinite <u>possibilities</u>. Since waves are the primary characteristic of all *potential possibilities*, which potential wave actually manifests into a particle (a photon, for example)? It could be any of them, but in both theory and in practice ***the greater the <u>probability</u> of a wave potential, the more likely it will be what actually manifests***.

So, what makes a particular wave more probable (likely) to manifest than another? A major factor in the wave probability equation is the ***strength or amplitude*** of the wave. Waves of greater amplitude have a higher probability of occurring. That is why very traumatic ***life experiences*** from past lives (or extremely positive life experiences for that matter) are more likely to occur (manifest locally in your current life) than other, less intense, experiences.[B2, C3, C4, C5]

Repetition is another aspect of this answer. There is an old saying, "Old habits die hard." The reason is that repetition (habit) increases the probability of the corresponding wave frequency actually manifesting (see 'Local Fields' later in this chapter). But learning new habits is also a matter of repetition (increasing the probability of a different wave frequency). It is ultimately a matter of ***conscious choice*** and consequently an important aspect of ***Conscious Living***.

Then there is the HUGE factor (actually, a necessary condition) of simply ***paying attention to*** (including observing, monitoring, measuring, etc.) events, people, thoughts, emotions, etc. in your life. This may occur unconsciously[B1, C7] or (especially) consciously as in ***Conscious Living***.[B1, C8, B2, C1] One excellent way to put this into practice is through ***conscious intention*** (see especially Chapter 5 and woven throughout subsequent chapters in the *Dancing with the Energy* books).

In terms of quantum physics, possibility waves with relatively high probabilities of actualizing are actually made stronger (even more probable) by observation (conscious intention, measurement, etc.). But this is also true of possibility waves with even relatively moderate or low probabilities! In short, observation acts as a 'booster shot' in terms of actualizing *any* possibility wave.

CONSCIOUSNESS—THE KEY TO MANIFESTATION

So then is light (remember that photon? or *any-thing else* for that matter) a particle or a wave? The answer is *"YES!"*

Remember, *the Matrix is pure energy with the <u>potential</u> to actualize (manifest) <u>infinite possibilities</u>*. All things being equal, some possibilities are more *probable* than others as previously discussed. The three books in the *Dancing with the Energy* series are about **Conscious Living**, which shows us how to *change the probabilities and how to strengthen possibility waves*—or more colloquially—how to stack the odds in our favor. **With Conscious Living, all things are <u>not</u> equal.** What??? How can this be???

Not surprisingly, the answer is, *"It's All About the Energy"* <u>**and**</u> **the Energy is all about <u>Consciousness</u>.** By the early 1930s, Max Planck, the "Father" of quantum physics, concluded that his equations and the experimental evidence available at the time pointed to consciousness as the basis of matter. In the past 20–30 years (as of this writing), the ill-defined and unquantifiable *quality* of consciousness has even more frequently taken center stage in the world of physics and, although often quite controversial in the scientific literature, it is nonetheless becoming a contemporary fixture in the scientific community.

Planck's work in quantum physics and his conclusion regarding consciousness were actually based on an experiment first conducted over a century before by Thomas Young (1773–1829; polymath and physician; *Experiments and Calculations Relative to Physical Optics*, 1804).

A century before that, Sir Isaac Newton (1642–1727; mathematician and physicist) published the final version of his theory of light as a *stream of particles* in his *Opticks* (1704). This idea actually goes back to the ancient wisdoms of Empedocles (c. 490–430 BCE; pre-Socratic philosopher) and ancient India (Samkhya school of Hinduism, early centuries CE).

While Newton's particle-theory of light prevailed for a century, Young's now-famous "double-slit experiment" *also* demonstrated the *wave theory* of light first proposed by Robert Hooke (1635–1703; natural philosopher, architect and polymath; *Micrographia,* "Observation XI," 1665). Planck's quantum theory (1900) was originally based on the wave-theory of light, but modern quantum physics has since demonstrated that light—and for that matter, *all energy—can be described with mathematical precision sometimes as particles and sometimes as waves.*

Continued replications and variations of Young's double-slit experiment have now demonstrated not only that waves of electromagnetic radiation can exist in more than one place simultaneously, but also that whether energy exists as waves or particles **depends on the observer (Consciousness)!** In short, modern physics has come to accept the conclusion that the observer is responsible for creating reality. Some contemporary physicists are even concluding that the universe itself is a "mental construction."

So, there you have it: *Matter is created by the observer, the consciousness that is <u>looking for</u> and <u>expecting</u> to see it.* On our own individual level (see Local Energy Fields later in this chapter), we literally create our own reality. Cultures and nations (shared local fields as described later) also create their own realities. Species (including *humans—Homo Sapiens*) also create their own realities. The question is whether we as a species, we as cultures, and *especially we as individuals <u>choose to take responsibility</u> for creating our present and future reality* from the unlimited potential of the Matrix or whether we *choose* to keep doing what we've always done, living the life that we have already created. *Remember, doing nothing is still a choice!*

"It's All About the Energy" <u>and</u> **the Energy is all about Consciousness.** But we have to learn to *use our consciousness correctly and efficiently in order to manifest what we desire both physically and spiritually while we are on the earth plane.* I call that process **Conscious Living**, and it is the central focus of the *Dancing with the Energy* series of books.

QUANTUM LOCALITY, NONLOCALITY, AND CORRELATION

Okay, so what is the difference between a particle and a wave of energy? *A wave is non-localized*, meaning that it can be in many places at once, some places being more probable or likely than others. *A particle, however, is localized*, meaning that it only can be in one place at a time. A particle is simply a quantum of wave energy (potential) that has been 'collapsed' (actualized) into manifestation through an *act of consciousness*.

You may have heard the term 'quantum leap' in casual conversation, usually referring to a big or sudden change in understanding, direction, etc. But a quantum leap is a real and important scientific phenomenon. It refers to an instantaneous change in *energy state* (amplitude) *without reference to space or time*, that is, in the Matrix.

For example, when an electron 'falls' from a 'higher' (energy) orbit around the nucleus of an atom to a 'lower' orbit, energy (in the form of light) is emitted. Similarly, an electron absorbs energy when it instantaneously 'leaps' to a higher orbit (higher energy state). Such quantum leaps are *nonlocal*. There is no 'space' through which the electron passes from one orbit to another. Nor is 'time' involved in the transfer; it is instantaneous. Nonlocal events occur only within the Unified Energy Field, the Matrix.

This is important because quanta (quantum objects or 'matter') experimentally have been shown to affect each other *outside of time and space* (nonlocality). There are no 'signals' between them and their mutual influence is instantaneous even when separated by very large distances where the time for light to travel can be precisely measured. Such objects (matter) are said to be 'correlated' and their mutual influence occurs nonlocally (in the Matrix) through prior interaction in the world of matter as discussed above. This is just a more complicated way of saying that *we live (locally) in at attraction-based Universe,* and that *the attraction resides (nonlocally) in the Matrix*.

That local interaction strengthens (increases) the probability of *potential interaction* (nonlocal—in the Matrix) manifesting in the world of (local) matter in the future *if we give our attention to it* (observe it, evaluate it, measure it, etc.) In other words, the brain is processing nonlocal information and we choose (consciously, unconsciously, or subconsciously) what actually manifests by observing (paying attention to) it. The more attention (in whatever form) we give it, the more likely it is to appear (become a 'reality') in our experience.

In summary, potential (nonlocal) waves differ in their probability of manifesting (locally) and *you can learn to change those probabilities to your liking*. Most importantly, a wave that has a lower probability of manifesting locally than another still can be manifested by a <u>willful</u> *act of consciousness*. That is what you learn to do with **Conscious Living**. *You can learn how to increase the likelihood of potential outcomes you want and to decrease the probability of manifesting outcomes you don't want*. In fact, you do it (unconsciously) all the time, day-by-day, moment-by-moment. The only question is whether you choose to take control of that process to create the life you desire or choose (by default—*unconsciously* choosing) to repeat old, past-life patterns and habits that you created and reinforced through the intensity and repetition of life experiences.

Simplified Translation: ***"Your thoughts create your reality."*** That is not just metaphysics, that's quantum physics. Changing your life begins with changing your thinking and continues with changing your beliefs and feelings. We shall take up these topics in subsequent chapters as well as in Books 2 and 3 of the *Dancing with the Energy* series.

Quantum Tangled Hierarchies

Since the correlation of possibility waves occurs in the matrix (the domain of potentialities outside of time and space), not only does the past influence the present and the future, the present (*NOW*) affects both the past and the future! What??? NOW affects the PAST? YES! Over a century ago Einstein told us that time is not linear at all. Today, physicists refer to "space-time" which Einstein showed (mathematically) to be curvilinear and subsequent experiments over the last century have confirmed. This interaction of events outside of time and space is known in quantum physics as a "tangled hierarchy" and the interesting thing is that the past, present, and future actually form a network of causes and effects that reinforce each other in the Matrix. In other words, they become stronger and, subsequently, more likely to manifest into one's experience of life.

For example, it has been shown experimentally using atoms that emit a pair of photons (particles of light). These photons are 'correlated' by virtue of their common origin. When the attributes of one photon are measured (observed by a consciousness) or changed, the other photon changes its attributes instantaneously no matter how far it is from the first photon. The only plausible explanation for this phenomenon is quantum nonlocality of tangled hierarchies. It is as if the photons are 'sharing' information that a human observer has measured (changed).

But the tangled hierarchy story doesn't end there. In another study, two people meditated together in a room for twenty minutes to establish 'correlated intentions.' They were then separated and placed in separate Faraday chambers (which block all electromagnetic signals) and instructed to continue meditating as before. One person was then shown a series of light flashes and their brain activity recorded by an EEG instrument. The other person's EEG activity was also recorded. When comparing the shape and strength of their brainwave activity, the two EEG recordings were very similar and at a level well above what would be expected by chance alone.

In the case of the photons, the correlation occurred through their physical interaction before they were emitted from the atom. But that 'correlation' was lost as soon as its possibility wave was 'collapsed' by measurement. For the meditators, however, correlation in brainwave activity was established through *conscious intention*. When they were isolated from each other in Faraday chambers, however, their brains remained correlated through their common intention. These experimental results demonstrate that *conscious intention alone* is all that is needed to 'correlate' two human brains so that what one person sees and responds to (brainwaves) can also be experienced by another person.

What does all this mean? It means that there is now a scientific basis for explaining such psychic phenomena as mental telepathy, soul memory, recognition of both friends and enemies from past lives, trapped energy of all sorts, chakras, remote energy healing, etc. which will be explored further in subsequent chapters. So, you see, ***"From the Ancient Wisdoms to Quantum Physics, It's All About the Energy!"***[B1, C2]

Fortunately for us, quantum tangled hierarchies provide both a tremendous opportunity and an excellent tool for becoming a better version of ourselves—soul evolution. The beautiful insights of quantum physics point directly to **consciousness** and **conscious intention** as the basis for healing the past, living more fully and joyously in the present, and creating the kind of future you desire as the end result. The means to those ends are both the subject and practice of **Conscious Living**.

VIBRATORY RESONANCE

The notion of resonance (an induced vibration that is the same or very similar in frequency to an external vibration) is widely recognized in physics in general (including music) and in quantum physics in particular (for example, in the notion of tangled hierarchies). In terms of the Ancient Wisdoms, the Book of Proverbs (23:7) in the *Bible* states: "As a man thinketh in his heart, so is he." Thus, one's thoughts and behavior tend to be quite consistent rather than wildly different.

In more recent times, this *Bible* verse became the basis of the metaphysical classic, *As A Man Thinketh* (1903), by James Allen (1864–1912; philosophical writer of inspirational books and poetry; pioneer of the self-help movement). In it he wrote that "A man is literally what he thinks, his character being the complete sum of all his thoughts" and many other similar ideas that today are generally referred to as the "*Law of Attraction*." Abraham-Hicks states repeatedly that *the universe responds not to what you desire, but to your current vibrational frequency. You attract experiences of a vibrational frequency that are similar to or resonate with your own.* It is literally the case that you are creating your own reality whether that 'reality' is what you want or not!

This last point is critical, because it isn't about karma or blaming other people for the less than desirable circumstances in which people often find themselves. It is important because ***it puts the power to become the Master of your life straight into your own hands***. This is the very core of Maitreya's teachings. It is also the quantum physics basis for practical applications[B3; C5] that can assist you in doing exactly that.

LOCAL FIELDS

The Matrix is sometimes referred to as the 'Unified Energy Field,' or simply 'The Field.' But researchers outside of quantum physics have also posited sub-fields of energy (local fields) that are shared by groups of individuals (similar resonant frequencies) as well as local fields specific to each of us as individuals.

The British biologist, Rupert Sheldrake (1942–; author, public speaker, and researcher in parapsychology), uses the term "morphic fields" to identify local fields that belong to all living cells, tissues, organs and organisms which shape and define each individual species. These morphic fields are habitual and become stronger each time they are repeated. Moreover, they are influenced by prior events, either for a species or for individuals, through a process he calls "morphic resonance." These individual-specific sub-fields of the Matrix permeate through and around the physical body (much like Patanjali's subtle bodies) and bear a striking resemblance to the notion of "tangled hierarchies."

For example, Sheldrake says that memory is intrinsic in nature, and that the members of "natural systems" inherit a "collective memory" from their ancestors. The implication is that an individual's behavior can be shaped by his or her prior experiences in their current life or from past lives (morphic resonance). People who share characteristics such as race, gender, religion, culture, etc. also tend to share attitudes and behaviors because their morphic fields 'resonate' with the morphic fields of similar individuals. Thus, morphic resonance is very similar to the notion of 'like attracts like', the foundation of the *"Law of Attraction"* (as expressed by Abraham) as well as the 'tangled hierarchies' of quantum physics.

In essence, local (including morphic) fields are energetic 'signatures' or characteristics based on patterns of the past. This concept also applies to learned behavior (for example, sociological patterns, customs, habits) as well as to instinctive behaviors. Morphic fields are said to impose rhythmic patterns on the nervous system, affecting the sensory and motor regions of the brain and thus behavior. Learned behaviors become established through *resonance with ourselves* and are strengthened through repetition (habit). I'll address this and the topic of changing such behaviors later in this chapter.

Morphic Resonance and Learning

Much of what is called 'learning' appears to be transmitted through the mechanism of morphic resonance. For example, a troop of baboons on a remote island figured out how to use simple tools to open coconuts, something that had never been observed previously in this species. Somehow, baboons thousands of miles away learned to do the same thing a generation later. Similarly, experiments with rats learning a maze resulted in an average of 165 errors per rat before they learned the maze. Thirteen generations later, however, their descendants learned the same maze with an average of only 20 errors. There are countless other examples in nature, including a number of migratory bird species who uncannily time their migration every year to arrive at exactly the time that food becomes available—even down to the migration of common swifts in Europe that arrive to feed on mayflies whose lifespan is literally a matter of only a few hours. At the time of this writing, something like morphic resonance with relevant subfields in the Matrix (tangled hierarchies) is the only plausible explanation for such mysteries.

Morphic Resonance and Memory

Memory has long been thought to be stored in the brain as 'material traces,' but countless experiments simply have not supported this notion. Francis Crick (1916–2004) a neuroscientist awarded the 1962 Nobel Prize in Medicine with James Watson (for their discovery of DNA in 1953), held that there is a practical issue with this idea. Except for the DNA inside the molecules of the brain, all of the brain's molecules are replaced within a matter of days or at most months, just as the molecules in all of the other parts of the body. Rupert Sheldrake suggests that our individual memories are actually stored in morphic fields when patterns of activity in the nervous system are similar to patterns of activity in the past. This is simply a matter of (morphic) *self-resonance*. Cell biologist Bruce Lipton (1944–; developmental biologist) discusses how each of the cells in your body has self-receptors that tune into the 'self' in the Matrix (not the Lower Self as described in this book but the individualized self—the Soul), an observation which is consistent both with Sheldrake's theory and with tangled hierarchies in quantum physics.

What about "soul memory" as it is sometimes called? While science has yet to identify or even define 'the soul.' research by Dr. Brian Weiss (1944–; psychiatrist, past-life therapist, and author) and others on past-life memories[B2, C5] provides increasing evidence pointing to the Matrix as their source. Thus, soul memories (tangled hierarchies) appear to be simply another form of vibrational resonance.

MORPHIC RESONANCE AND EMOTIONAL FIELDS

As noted previously[B1, C2], emotions are energy, and the concept of morphic fields can also be applied to emotions. Most of us have 'felt' a tangible difference between 'vibrations' of anger and love emanating from other people that go far beyond their overt behavior alone. Emotions of all kinds are vibrational frequencies that we not only experience internally, we also emanate or 'send out' these frequencies into our external environment. Anger, for example, has a much lower vibrational frequency than love, with most other emotions falling between these two obvious extremes. When you raise your vibrational frequency, you are better ***Aligned*** with Source Energy.

Because morphic resonance is strengthened by repetition, habit, and consciously trying to develop and experience a higher emotional frequency, it provides a relatively easy and effective tool for slowly moving oneself up the emotional scale. This minimizes the tendency to fall back to a lower emotional (vibrational) state. In other words, even though we are creatures of habit, those habits can systematically be changed. I will discuss this topic later in this chapter as well as in greater detail later.[B1, C4, C6]

MORPHIC RESONANCE AND DISEASE FIELDS

Just like any other manifestation of energy, diseases have their own morphic fields. These fields are said to be 'downloaded' from the collective consciousness of those who have gone through the same or a similar disease in the past. To this, one then adds their personal beliefs, fears, etc., and then repeats the associated behavioral patterns (forming habits) associated with that disease (morphic resonance). Those who manage to overcome 'incurable' conditions have altered their point of attraction (what they are thinking about) to resonate with a different morphic field and thus are able to heal. Once again, the key to changing one's physical condition is changing the energy of their morphic fields.

YOU CAN CHANGE YOUR EXPERIENCE OF LIFE

Now we can add perhaps the most important and exciting addition to the list of basic points regarding quantum physics and the Matrix: *You can change how you experience life by consciously working to change your local morphic fields (energy) in the Matrix.* This promises the potential ability to heal yourself at every level, to experience a more full and joyful life, and to help you in the process of soul evolution.

This point is critical because it puts the power to become the Master of your life directly into your own hands. This is the very core of Maitreya's teachings as well as those of Abraham-Hicks. It is also the quantum physics basis for practical applications that can assist you in doing exactly that. I'll address these in greater detail in Books 2 and 3 of *Dancing with the Energy*.

Quantum Physics and the Ancient Wisdoms

The system of subtle bodies[B1, C3] is attributed to the *Vedas*, a collection of spiritual and religious texts originating about 2,500–3,000 years ago. The Indian sage, Patanjali (circa 5th to 2nd century BCE philosopher and author), proposed four energy fields or "subtle bodies"[B1, C3] that generate and govern the chakras. Without going into detail, the Table 4-1 briefly describes their relationship to quantum fields.

Table 4-1
Relationships Between the Subtle Bodies of the Ancient Wisdoms, Quantum Physics, and Local Fields

Ancient Wisdoms	Quantum Physics and Local Fields (Tangled Hierarchies)
Spiritual Body	Universal Energy Field (the Matrix), including relationships with other souls
Mental Body	Local fields related to current and past-life (soul) memories: culture, beliefs, etc.
Emotional Body	Local emotional fields including current and past-life emotions
Etheric Body	Local fields relating to current and past-life disease and physical conditions

Changing Behaviors and Habits

As stated earlier, local fields are energy sub-fields (generated by tangled hierarchies) in the Matrix that are either shared by groups of people (for example, race, gender, religion, culture) or that are specific to each individual. These local or "morphic" fields not only shape and define the cells, tissues, and organs of all living organisms, they also mold and define us as individual human beings (for example, learning, memory, emotions, diseases). These factors ultimately contribute to forming and determining our individual behaviors and habits.

But what about choice and free will? Are we simply 'victims' of our morphic fields, held for ransom by the energies that make up every atom and vibration of our being? Well, "Yes" and "No." Of course, we can always change our minds at any time about what we'll have for dinner tonight—even if we have to make a special trip to the market or a specific restaurant in order to satisfy our particular gustatory whims of the moment!

What about behaviors that have strong consequences such as violating social customs or breaking the law? We still have a choice, but we are more likely to consider the consequences of our choice *before* engaging in the behavior. And if we feel that we have no choice—the behavior in question is just too extreme given the consequences—well, we've still made a choice! It may not be what we want to do, but we choose to do it anyway because the consequences are just too severe if we don't do it. Such influences on our behavior clearly derive from one or more of the morphic fields discussed previously. Our choices of behaviors 'resonate' with the morphic fields of our culture, legal environment, social groups, etc. So, do we really have a choice?

And what about behaviors for which the legal or social consequences are weak or nonexistent, but which we just can't seem to change no matter how hard we try? In other words, what about our personal 'habits?' Well, these behaviors are also influenced by morphic fields—our own! At any given moment in time, we resonate more strongly with our own morphic fields than with those from any other source. The more we repeat any behavior, the stronger its morphic field becomes. At some point, the morphic resonance becomes just too great a force for 'willpower.' Habits trump willpower most of the time.

Paramhansa Yogananda has often been quoted as saying that "Environment is stronger than willpower." This is true even of our own personal habits because the choice to engage or not engage in habitual behaviors is (a) largely unconscious and (b) even when we do think about it, the choice is almost always in the context of our social (morphic) environment.

So, do we ever really have a choice? At the end of the day, we really are 'hostage' even to our own habits, aren't we? The answer is likely "Yes," *if* we just keep beating our heads against the wall of habit, failing time after time to permanently change our behavior. *But the answer can be "No" if we choose to change the energy in the relevant local morphic fields of the matrix!*

Maitreya teaches that we are here on the earth plane to learn to become the Master of our own life. In other words, we must learn not to be prisoners of social and cultural conditioning as well of as our own emotions and habits. Maitreya, Yogananda, and many other spiritual teachers advise us to surround ourselves with good company, good books, etc., because they know that *environment really is stronger than willpower*. So, what to do?

Changing your external environment absolutely helps, but ***changing your internal environment is essential***. Spiritually speaking, that process is called *"transformation,"* changing your current vibrational frequency to a higher vibrational frequency. That is what **Conscious Living** is about. But how can you change your *internal environment*? Let's examine this a bit more.

CHANGING BEHAVIORAL FIELDS

As stated previously, the more a behavior is repeated, the stronger its morphic field becomes and the more we resonate with it. We can't very reliably just 'will' a change in habitual behavior. We have to work to change the energy in the relevant morphic fields—*replace* the old energy with an entirely new energy—if we hope to have any real chance of success. The conscious mind simply does not override either the subconscious mind or the local fields that influence it. The British biologist, Rupert Sheldrake writes of "changing your tuning" from one local field to another. In other words, rather than unconsciously 'tuning' into one morphic field through habit, we can tune into a different morphic field *if we choose to do so*. Thus, **conscious intention** to create and/or immerse ourselves in an environment that is more supportive of the new behavior can be an incredibly effective tool in changing habits.

The key concept here is '*changing the tuning*.' It has often been said, "Energy goes where attention flows." By tuning-in to a new field that supports a change in behavior, we *feel* differently. We are likely to feel more confident in actually changing the behavior because the new field has its own resonance. But if we think too soon that we have 'beat the old habit' before the new field becomes stronger than the old one, we are likely to slide back and ultimately fail because the old field *initially is* stronger than the new one.

Chapter 4: Human Energy Fields and Quantum Physics

So, what's the solution? Remember the points regarding quantum physics discussed previously:

- We send our thoughts out into the Matrix and those thoughts are attracted back to us as life experiences.

- We can change how we experience life by changing our local morphic fields (energy) in the Matrix.

It is almost axiomatic in contemporary metaphysical literature that "your thoughts create your reality," and this view is supported by quantum physics. But does simply changing your thoughts really work? And if so, how does it happen? Isn't there more to it than just changing your thoughts? What do you have to do to make it work more effectively? These are important questions which I will deal with later in greater detail.[B1, C5, C6; B2, C1; & especially B3, C5]

Summary of Human Energy Fields and Quantum Physics

- Matter (including your body) is made up of energy vibrating so fast that it appears to be solid.

- Everything (including you) is linked by an energetic web known as the Matrix.

- The Matrix is pure energy with the potential to manifest infinite possibilities from which you, as a conscious being, are able to choose—*if* you learn how *and* choose to do so.

- You send your thoughts out into the Matrix and, through the principle of *resonance* (or "*Law of Attraction*" if you prefer), those thoughts are attracted back to you as life experiences.

- You can change how you experience life by changing the energy of your local (morphic) fields in the Matrix to resonate with (attract) different outcomes.

Conscious Living and Quantum Physics

Remember, the ability to change how you experience life by changing your local morphic fields (energy) in the Matrix promises the potential to heal yourself at every level of the human experience. In addition, it opens the door to a new way of changing not only your old habits, but also a way to assist the process of transformation, raising your vibrational frequency to a new level of consciousness. The Matrix has the *potential* to manifest literally anything—*if* you learn how to *Allow* your energy to flow unhindered, *Balance* the energies of life, and *Align* those energies with Higher Self—Source Energy.

Conscious Living gives you the power to become the Master of your life. This is the very core of Maitreya's, Abraham's, and Yogananda's teachings (as well as many others). It is also the quantum physics basis for everything I'll be discussing later in the *Dancing with the Energy* books.

Chapter 5: The Power of Your Thoughts

Introduction

Chapter 4 introduced the scientific evidence for the often-quoted 'New Age' idea that "your thoughts create your reality." The topic of thoughts seems so mundane and obvious that one might wonder why it is necessary to devote an entire chapter to the subject. Well, if it were so obvious, why is it that almost all of us spend so much time dwelling on negative thoughts? It's not like this is a new idea—the Ancient Wisdoms were well aware of it, and down through the ages people from all walks of life have recognized the power of our thoughts.

- "One comes to be of just such stuff as that on which the mind is set." ~ *Upanishads* (6th century BCE Sanskrit texts)

- "All that is, is the result of what we have thought."... "Your worst enemy cannot harm you as much as your own unguarded thoughts." ... "***We are what we think***. All that we are arises with our thoughts. With our thoughts we make the world. Speak or act with a pure mind and

85

happiness will follow as your shadow, unshakable." ~ Gautama Buddha (c. 563–483 BCE; spiritual teacher and founder of Buddhism)

- "They are able who *think* they are able." ~ Virgil (70–19 BCE; Roman epic poet)

- "Such as are your *habitual thoughts*, such also will be the character of your mind; for the soul is dyed by the thoughts." ~ Marcus Antoninus Aurelius (CE 121–180; Emperor of Rome 161–180, Stoic philosopher)

- "A man is what he *thinks* about all day long." ~ Ralph Waldo Emerson (1803–1882; philosopher and writer)

Since the middle of the twentieth century, some of the greatest scientific minds have also become profoundly aware of the importance of thought (and especially *consciousness*) as the fundamental basis of energy, matter, and the processes of creation and manifesting. It has now become part and parcel of contemporary physical science as well as modern metaphysics.

Conscious Thoughts

Your conscious thoughts are the most important, most practically useful, and the most powerful form of energy you have at your disposal, for every purpose, including soul evolution. ***Why are they the most important form of energy?***

- "YOU are creating every day what you want in your life—*your thoughts and your fears are creating YOUR world*. The more you think positively, the more you think of a peaceful world, the more you will create it!" ~ Maitreya (Newsletter #309, April 9, 2010)

Chapter 5: The Power of Your Thoughts

Your thoughts are also the ***most powerful form of energy*** you have at your disposal because you—and you alone—think your thoughts, and they determine your experience of every aspect of your life. They are the ***most practically useful form of energy*** because ***you*** **have power over your mind**, *not* outside events. You have no control over what other people are thinking or doing, the economy, politics, etc., but you *can* have complete control over your thoughts *if* you choose to take on that responsibility. But that is a habit, and one that relatively few people accept. In a universe governed by the *Law of Attraction*, what you consistently think is what you get, and you have the power to think what you choose. As James Allen put it so beautifully in his book, *As a Man Thinketh* (1903):

- "Mind is the Master-power that molds and makes,
And Man is Mind, and evermore he takes
The tool of Thought, and shaping what he wills,
Brings forth a thousand joys, a thousand ills.
He thinks in secret and it comes to pass;
Environment is but his looking-glass."

Let's face it, the power of thought we human beings have evolved/created is the most complex and complete—albeit imperfect—form of consciousness on this planet. We are inherently creatures of thought, but the vast majority of the species has little or no idea of the power, responsibility, and opportunity this fact places in our own hands.

I believe it is fair to say that *unconscious living* is by far the norm in human affairs. ***Conscious Living*** is the key to successful living in any realm—material, physical, emotional, or spiritual.[B1, C2] The challenge for each individual is ***learning how to use the energies of life*** to your best advantage to become the

Master of YOUR life and to create the life YOU desire. How do you do this?

Chapter 2 outlined a hierarchy of three *General Principles of Energy as the fundamental basis of all energy work—Alignment, Balance, and Allowing the energy to flow*. To review: You can't *Balance* your energy without *Allowing* it to flow unhindered, and you can't *Align* with Higher Self without *Balancing* your energy. If you want to achieve *Alignment/ Harmony*, you must begin the process with the basics—Allowing the energy of YOUR Higher Self to flow freely without resistance.

How do you do that? You start with your thoughts. As we have just seen, your conscious thoughts are the most important, most practically useful, and the most powerful form of energy you have at your conscious disposal. But there is an *even more powerful form of thought* you need to consider as well.

Beliefs

What is a 'Belief?' Various dictionaries define a belief as an opinion or conviction in which one has confidence, faith, or trust. In contrast, a 'thought' is defined simply as the product of mental activity, or that which one thinks; an idea or notion. Thought includes the concept of intention, design, or purpose, especially a half-formed or imperfect intention. Intention[B1, C4] is clearly more potent than just a random or run-of-the-mill 'thought,' but it is also clear that a 'belief' goes farther yet. Above all, beliefs are thoughts that we regard as being true, without regard to other factors.

In essence, *your beliefs are your thoughts on steroids*.

Chapter 5: The Power of Your Thoughts

- "One person with a belief is equal to a force of 99 who have only interests." ~ John Stuart Mill (1806–1873; economist and philosopher)

Because of their strength, we need to be particularly watchful regarding our beliefs. For example, psychologists (and many others) have long known that our *perceptions* are often based not on objective evidence, but rather are formed to be *consistent with our beliefs*. In other words, our beliefs can, and often do, distort what we 'see' and 'hear' from our environment.

- "People only see **what they are prepared to see** [what they believe]." ~ Ralph Waldo Emerson

Or as Robert Oxton Bolton (1572–1631; clergyman and academic) put it: "A belief is not merely an idea the mind possesses; it is an idea that possesses the mind." Another way of saying this is that beliefs begin with thoughts, but eventually they replace the conscious thought processes so prized by human beings. In short, our beliefs tell us what to see. They pacify us (the comfort zone) and they satisfy us ("I am *right*"—or is it "I am *righteous*?"). Ultimately, **what we believe is what we experience**.

When and from where did your personal beliefs originate? Examine them carefully. To what extent are they formed from the process of *conditioning* rather than from your own observations and reflection? Have some of them simply become 'habits' (actually, *self-conditioning*) that reflect more of your personal comfort zone than what resonates with your Higher Self? It has long been observed that if a lie is repeated frequently enough, people will eventually believe it, to *accept it as their truth*. There is absolutely nothing wrong with *your truth*, as long as it is actually true!

- "What gets us into trouble is not what we don't know. It's what we know for sure that just ain't so." ~ attributed to Mark Twain (1835–1910; pen name of Samuel Langhorne Clemens, humorist, novelist, short story author, and wit)

The point is that our beliefs have the very strong potential to bind us to a rigid and unyielding view of the world around us and of ourselves. This is the antithesis—the direct opposite—of the ***Principle of Alignment with Higher Self***. It is contractive, not expansive. It feels like resistance, not allowance. It doesn't admit growth and change, but fosters entrenchment and rigidity.

It is also the opposite of the ***Principle of Balance*** because it invites us to ready—and often premature—***judgment*** of what is 'right' versus what is 'wrong' even well-before we have bothered to consider the possibility—let alone validity—of another point of view.

- "No soul has the right to say what is right or wrong. Only the energy known as God can do that, and even then, God does not judge, but gently shows where you have taken the wrong road or made the wrong decision." ~ Maitreya (Newsletter #77, July 6, 2003)

In other words, *judgment is ultimately condemnation*, and that just isn't the nature of your Higher Self or of Source energy. It is completely the opposite of ***Alignment***, and derails every effort to achieve it. It certainly isolates us from others and their opinions through our own fear and doubt, violating the *Principle of **Allowing** Source Energy to Flow freely* through every aspect of our beings. We only *allow* within the limits of our beliefs.

The Self is very much aware of our beliefs and very effectively uses them against us to stifle and even to stop our intellectual and spiritual growth. It keeps us in a narrow and 'safe' comfort zone that doesn't allow the consideration of alternative perspectives, let alone the possibility that we, ourselves, might be in error. In addition, the Self assists us in digging our own hole deeper through self-justification and rejection of anything contrary to what we believe.

It has been said that, "We all get the God we believe in." Think about how often humankind justifies its own beliefs and actions by invoking God as being on 'our side' and not on 'their side.' Really? It all depends on whose 'God' we believe—and, of course, it is *always* our own!

To reiterate: our beliefs have the very strong potential to bind us to a rigid and unyielding view of the world around us and of ourselves—*if* we allow them to do so. *But we get to choose our thoughts and we also get to choose whether to put those thoughts on steroids, thus choosing our beliefs. That is the process of* **Conscious Living.**

So, how do you develop functional and beneficial beliefs? ***By practicing the repetition of positive, uplifting, and beneficial thoughts not only about the world around you, but also about yourself.*** Thoughts repeated often enough and long enough become beliefs. Those positive beliefs actually become a part of the 'energy signature' of every physical cell in your body as well as your emotional life. ***You can literally change your life by changing your beliefs***. So, let's put your thoughts and beliefs to work!

Tips for Effectively Utilizing Your Thoughts

TIP #1 – ALIGN YOUR THOUGHTS WITH HIGHER SELF

This principle was introduced earlier[B1, C2] as *Align/Harmonize with Higher-Self Energy*, by far the most important of the three Energy Principles. Since your thoughts (and beliefs) are the most important, most practically useful, and the most powerful form of energy you have at your disposal, this principle is essential whether you are interested in soul evolution or not. Most of the time, nearly every one of us *unconsciously Aligns* our lives to the energy of the Self through habit, conditioning, fear, and doubt. That is why a concerted effort toward **Conscious Living** is so essential, and it begins with your thoughts and beliefs.

TIP #2 – FOCUS YOUR ATTENTION

"Energy goes where attention flows." Is this just some 'New Age' mumbo jumbo or is there scientific evidence to support it? As we saw in the previous chapter, waves of energy become particles when they are measured or observed—in other words, when we *consciously pay attention to them*. So, even quantum physics tells us that energy follows attention. You are far more likely to achieve what you want to achieve when you focus all your attention on one thing rather than scattering your attention over many things. That is pretty obvious, but _how_ *you focus your attention* is often not so obvious.

The single most important aspect of _how_ you focus is summed up in what is called the *Law of Attraction*. There are many people who disparage this universal law, complaining that "It doesn't work," but when one compares what they _say_ *they are doing* with what *they actually are doing*, it becomes clear pretty quickly that they really don't understand it. Misunderstanding and misapplication provide little basis for condemnation and complaint. Abraham-Hicks has a formal definition for this law: "That which is like unto itself is drawn." To put it very simply, "*Like attracts like.*" We will be revisiting this universal law frequently later in this series of books.

In terms of the energy tip of *Focusing Your Attention*, the *Law of Attraction* tells us to *focus on what you want, NOT on what you don't want*. In other words:

- If you want to manifest money, don't focus on how little is in your checking account. Focus (with appreciation) on the abundance you already enjoy in your life and how wonderful it feels to have even more money showing up in your bank account. Focus on enjoying abundance, not complaining about its lack.

- If you want to heal from an illness or injury, don't focus on your pain and suffering. Focus on how much better you feel day-by-day, hour-by-hour, and the wonderful feeling of health and well-being you enjoy when you are well or healed. Focus on feeling good, not on feeling your pain.

- If you want to stop smoking, don't focus on cancer, emphysema, or how many dozens of times you've tried to stop smoking but failed. Focus on how good it feels to breathe freely and to clear your lungs and body of the chemical poisons in tobacco smoke. Focus on health and success, not on fear of sickness and death.

- If you want to run your first marathon, don't focus on how hard it will be and how exhausted you will feel in doing it.

Focus on the exhilaration of crossing the finish line and the sense of satisfaction and achievement at your accomplishment. Focus on success, not on fatigue and pain.

- And if you want to raise your level of consciousness, don't focus on what you might have to give up (for example, the possessions you might need to get rid of, the 'friends' you might lose, the hard work you will have to do on your own lessons, karma, past-life 'stuff'). Focus instead on the lessons you have already learned, the wisdom you have already gained through your experience, and the wonderful feeling of well-being you enjoy when you are in **Alignment/ Harmony** with your Higher Self. Focus on progress toward Higher Self and well-being, not on difficulty and the loss of things that bind you to the Self.

Notice that everything you <u>want</u> in this list is expressed in the *present tense*, even if you don't have it or don't feel it just yet. *This is <u>very</u> important*, and I will discuss the "Secrets of Manifesting" in much greater detail in a later book in the *Dancing with the Energy* series.[B3, C5] In short, **refuse to think about what you fear and the things you don't want in your life**.

The *Law of Attraction* is really quite simple, and yet very difficult to learn to practice consistently. We are accustomed to complaining about our health, our jobs, our friends, etc. rather than appreciating their good qualities. *We tend to complain about what we don't have rather than appreciating what we do have.* As I said previously, 'Old habits die hard.' It takes considerable practice to use this universal law correctly, but you will find that **always** seeking to **Align** your energy with your Higher Self and focusing on that end goal is the easiest way to make a good habit of effectively using the *Law of Attraction* to your benefit.

OK, so everybody already *knows this*. So what? What's the big deal? Well, it is the most successful people in every department of life who *practice it* every day of their lives. Focus of attention is absolutely necessary to **Allowing** the energy to flow, thereby **Balancing** your energies, and achieving **Alignment** with Your Higher Self. Remember, if you **believe** that you can attain or achieve anything you desire and **stay focused on your goal**, you will be guided and assisted by Spirit in the process of learning to become a better version of yourself.

TIP #3 – STATE YOUR INTENTION CLEARLY

As stated previously, *energy follows **attention***. However, even more energy follows ***intention***. The best way to focus your attention on anything you desire is to express it in the form of an intention, a purpose, an objective, a goal. To put it plainly, *intention is critical* no matter what it is you want to create or manifest.

There is overwhelming, long-standing scientific evidence in the psychological and management literature that performance goals—intentions—are far more effective if they are:
- *Specific* (quantifiable) vs. general (for example, 'do your best')
- *Difficult* but attainable
- *Accepted* by the performer

Such goals consistently produce the highest levels of performance regardless of the task involved. (Mento, A. J.; Steel, R. P.; Karren, R. J., 1987. "A meta-analytic study of the effects of goal setting on task performance: 1966–1984." *Organizational Behavior and Human Decision Processes*, 39: 52)

It is no different whether one is trying to raise their level of consciousness, lose weight, or improve their bowling score. A specific goal defines a desired level of achievement, and a difficult goal mobilizes greater effort to attain it, but only if the goal is accepted by the individual. One might think that any goal a person sets for themselves would automatically be 'accepted,' but this is not necessarily the case. Many people purposely set unrealistically high goals so that, when they fail to attain them, they can more easily blame outside factors rather than their own effort. When the going gets tough, genuine or sincere 'commitment' to goal attainment is often required for success. This is the point at which genuine *belief* in your thoughts and intentions becomes even more important. Ultimately, it is all about *Alignment*.

TIP #4 – TRANSFORM YOUR THOUGHTS INTO BELIEFS

Truly believing in your thoughts gives them power because it invests them with a qualitatively more potent energy. They resonate with you as 'true,' and you tend to cling to them avidly, whether or not they actually benefit you materially, emotionally, or (especially) spiritually.

Chapter 7 will discuss the conscious mind and the subconscious mind, how they interact, and how each of them affects—and is affected by—your thoughts. In terms of Tip #4, it is important to understand that here I am talking about *working with your conscious mind to influence and to reprogram your subconscious mind*. How can you best do that?

Earlier[B1, C2] I discussed three major Principles of Energy, *Alignment/Harmony*, *Balance*, and *Allowing* the Energy to Flow. In terms of thoughts, *beliefs are all about Allowing* because you regard your own beliefs as true. As such, you generally offer little or no resistance to your beliefs. You accept them implicitly and thus *Allow* the Energy of Source, your Higher Self, to flow unhindered through you.

Chapter 5: The Power of Your Thoughts

Remember, your beliefs are your thoughts on steroids. If your beliefs are in *Alignment* with Higher Self, then you are *Allowing*. If your beliefs are in *alignment* with the Self, then you are not *allowing*, but *resisting alignment* with Higher Self.

PROVIDE SUPPORT FOR YOUR THOUGHTS

Paramhansa Yogananda was often quoted as saying that "Environment is stronger than willpower." His meaning is quite straightforward and obvious, but there is a flip side to this phrase as well. *You can learn to use your external environment to your advantage—to support your conscious intentions.* Through applying the principles of **Conscious Living**, you can overcome the oft-used reason (really just an 'excuse') that "*I have no willpower.*" The fact is, *you do have the power if you have the will (intention) and do what is necessary to support it.* You have the *choice* 'to do or not to do' as you wish; that power is *yours*.

As noted in Tip #2, the single most important aspect of *how* you focus your attention is the **Law of Attraction.** If you intend to transform your thoughts into beliefs, you must *purposely* surround yourself with support from your outside environment (for example, people, your physical environment, supportive resources) as well as *purposely* work to put your thoughts and intentions on steroids (beliefs). A supportive environment for your thoughts will go a long way toward helping you to establish them as beliefs—thoughts you regard as implicitly true on their own merit. But there are other things you can do as well.

CONSCIOUSLY AND FREQUENTLY REPEAT YOUR THOUGHTS

How best to do this? *Affirmations*. This topic is so important that I devote an entire chapter to it later.[B3, C3] Affirmations are

97

so easy to use—and even easier to *misuse*—that many people dismiss them as not being worthwhile. But properly used, affirmations can definitely help to create beliefs from your thoughts.

- "Belief consists in accepting the *affirmations* of the soul; unbelief in denying them." ~ Ralph Waldo Emerson

Whether a statement is true or false, **repetition leads to belief. Affirmations are statements of what you want in your life as if they were already true.** The old saying, "Fake it until you make it" is quite literally true. Until you come to *believe* your affirmations, they will likely not have sufficient power to manifest in your life (think of amplitude, or 'signal strength' required to collapse a wave of possibility into actuality).[B1, C4]

GIVE YOUR THOUGHTS EMOTIONAL POWER

Chapter 6 will discuss the powerful effect of emotions on your life, how to deal with them effectively, and how to use them to your advantage. In the present context, however, there is wide agreement that beliefs having a strong emotional feeling behind them are far more powerful than when they are not accompanied by strong emotional feeling. Again, think of amplitude in increasing the probability of collapsing possibility into matter).

Negative or neutral feelings can sabotage your best efforts, making them useless, while genuinely positive emotional feelings energize your affirmations and thoughts with sincerity. This **sincerity of positive feelings Allows and empowers trust**, the cornerstone of belief. Make giving your affirmations this emotional power a habit and you will achieve results much faster.

- "You limit yourselves in so many ways. However, once you *believe* that abundance is yours and that it can be used to help others, then it will surely come into your life." ~ Maitreya (Newsletter #312, April 19, 2010)

Tip #5 – Balance Your Thoughts

Remember, **Balancing** is the process of restoring your energies to their natural state, that is, **Alignment** with Higher Self. In some respects, the *Law of Attraction* instructs us to **balance** our thoughts by focusing on what we want rather than on what we don't want in order to **eliminate negative energies** from the body, mind, and spirit so that all that is left is positive. But there is still more to balance when it comes to **Balancing** your thoughts.

What does it mean to "**Balance your thoughts**?" One of the meanings of the word *'balance'* has to do with steadiness, stability, constancy, or consistency. *Balance* in this sense is critical to effectively using your thoughts to achieve your life goals in any department of life. For example, most people who try using affirmations[B3, C3] don't use them consistently. They only do it when they happen to think about it rather than programming it into their daily schedule. Or they try using affirmations (albeit with good intentions) for only a few days or weeks before giving up.

Consistency, constancy, steadfastness of purpose—in other words, **Balance**—is required for success in any area of life, and especially when it comes to raising your consciousness. If you want to transform your thoughts into powerful beliefs, you ***must work at it consistently***.

- "Some men give up their designs when they have almost reached the goal, while others, on the contrary, obtain a victory by exerting, at the last moment, more vigorous efforts than ever before." ~ Herodotus (c. 484–c. 425 BCE; historian regarded as the "Father of History" in Western culture)

Summary of Tips for Effectively Utilizing Your Thoughts

- Tip #1 – Align Your Thoughts with Higher Self
- Tip #2 – Focus Your Attention
- Tip #3 – State Your Intention Clearly
- Tip #4 – Transform Your Thoughts into Beliefs
- Tip #5 – Balance Your Thoughts

Conscious Living and Thoughts

The practice of **Conscious Living** recognizes the incontrovertible fact that your thoughts create your reality, and that *you get to choose what thoughts will occupy your mind, your time, and your life*. If you want to accomplish anything in any area of life, you must consciously begin with your thoughts. But that is just the beginning. We now turn to Chapter 6, "Managing Your Emotions," to continue our investigation of how to become the Master of your life.

Chapter 6: Managing Your Emotions

Introduction

We human beings like to think of ourselves as masters of rational thought, but as we have seen previously, this is not really the case. We are masters of rationalizing and distorting our 'rational' thought processes. In fact, the world of emotions is really where we live most of our time day or night. Our 'rational' thought processes work fairly well as long as they are congruent with our feelings but, when there is a conflict between what we think and what we feel, our emotions tend to win the contest most of the time.

Think about your likes and dislikes. For example, why do you prefer one model of automobile over another? Certainly, there are many 'rational' thoughts involved (for example, fuel mileage, safety ratings, economics), but there are many 'irrational' thoughts as well (for example, style, fit with self-image, perceived prestige of ownership). Whatever your reasons, preferences (likes and dislikes) boil down to emotional responses. And what about your preferences for clothing? Don't most of those 'reasons' for your choices have to do with emotions? And what about the interpersonal relationship we call 'love?' Such relationships very often form, and even continue over many years, in spite of all the 'rational' (actually 'rationalizing') reasons people frequently generate.

Emotions are clearly much of what not only makes us human, but also much of what makes us distinct as individual human beings. However, only a little reflection obviously will tell us that emotions can be as problematic as thoughts at times. Strong emotions, like strong beliefs, can easily lead us to fool ourselves.

Nonetheless, I believe that *both* thoughts *and* emotions are a necessary and indispensable part of our humanity. But we need to learn *how* to use *both* of them constructively and effectively to our advantage if we hope to benefit our lives from either of them. This is the business of **Conscious Living**.

Emotions and Emotional States

Many emotions begin with thoughts, whether conscious or subconscious.[B1, C7] But not all thoughts produce any real effect on our lives. Thoughts that do not stir up emotion within us have little or no real power behind them. In order for thoughts to have any real power, there must be an emotional or feeling response, and the stronger the emotion (either positive or negative), the more it affects both our thoughts and behaviors.

An emotion is a feeling response that accompanies a belief (a thought) with which we identify or to which we are attached. When a strong emotion (either positive or negative) is involved, we often hold onto it (repress it, bottle it up), and it gets 'stuck' in the Emotional Body. It is the inability to detach from the belief or the emotion that prevents the energy of Source from flowing

Chapter 6: Managing Your Emotions

through us naturally, violating the third major *Energy Principle of Allowing*.

In the first chapter of this book, I discussed the Levels of Human Consciousness or Awareness. Figure 6-1 illustrates the emotional highs and lows one tends to experience over time at the lower levels of awareness, often extending into the early stages of Solar Consciousness. I have chosen to label this pattern of emotional swings over time as 'Emotional States in Unconscious Living' which are often characterized as a 'Roller Coaster' or sometimes as typical of a 'Drama Queen.'

**Figure 6-1
Emotional States in Unconscious Living
(Roller Coaster)**

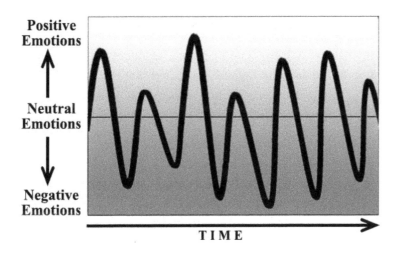

The point here is that a large proportion of the population tends to display a wide range of emotional states, bouncing around between emotional highs and lows. These fluctuations are largely driven by what is going on in their subconscious mind[B1, C7] and/or by the external environment in which they find themselves at the moment.

The behavior of those in unconscious living is largely controlled by their emotional responses to their environment rather than their conscious choices. There is nothing inherently wrong with this state of affairs as it allows one easily to blame their negative emotions on their environment and attribute their moments of happiness to external events, other people, and to 'things' (for example, possessions, social status). In fact, it can be a comfortable alternative as it requires little responsibility either for one's immediate situation or indeed, one's own life. Many people, however, have sought what they believe to be a 'better' way to approach life.

For example, among the Ancient Wisdoms, the Stoic philosophers gave primary importance to controlling the emotions. Stoicism is a school of Greek philosophy founded in the early 3rd century BCE by Zeno of Athens. It taught that virtue based on knowledge is the highest good, and that the wise are indifferent to the changes of fortune experienced in everyday life as well as being indifferent to both pleasure and pain.

Figure 6-2 illustrates the Stoic philosophers' vision of the ideal wise man's 'Calm Indifference' to human emotions. Note the narrow range of emotional intensity hovering closely around a relatively tranquil neutral emotional state.

Chapter 6:Managing Your Emotions

**Figure 6-2
Emotional States in Stoicism
(Calm Indifference)**

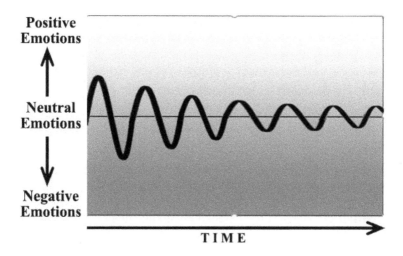

Without delving into a lengthy philosophical discussion, the following summary accurately portrays the essence of Stoicism:

- The ideal state of mind is tranquility that fosters a calm indifference to everything in one's life
- Happiness is unsustainable, so just be 'virtuous'

On the other hand, the critiques of Stoicism have been many and persistent. Jane Austen (1775–1817; novelist) in her novel, *Sense and Sensibility* (1811), accurately summarizes the Stoic teachings: "Always resignation and acceptance. Always prudence and honour and duty. Elinor, where is your heart?" This can lead to a 'starving' of the emotions resulting in a humorless and rigid personality.

In short, the Stoics essentially *denied* their emotions under the guise of *non-attachment* when, in fact, they simply refused to express them or to deal with them in a healing or constructive manner. I will discuss both denial and repression of emotions later in this chapter and in subsequent *Dancing with the Energy* books.

Emotions and Conscious Living

When an emotion (energy with which we identify or to which we are attached) remains unused or unexpressed (including denial and repression), that energy becomes stagnant, poisonous.[B1, C4] It festers in the emotional body, keeps us from raising our consciousness, and causes problems in the other subtle bodies as well as the physical body. Examples of such emotional energies include anger, resentment, frustration, abandonment, fear, doubt, low self-esteem, etc.

Maitreya has written extensively about such emotions:

- "I have been asked on more than one occasion about emotions. What are they and how do they affect our spiritual lives? First of all, I must emphasize that, when I am writing about emotions, I am referring to *negative emotions* such as anger, etc. The emotional body is a part of humanity tied to the animal part of you. It is a part of the Self, a separate body which is designed to hold you back from moving forward. It knows all your fear, anger, frustration, weak, negative parts of you, and it is capable of pulling it out of a hat like magic whenever it needs to slow you down." ~ Maitreya (Newsletter #256, November 2, 2009)

In other newsletters, Maitreya frequently writes about emotions and the emotional body. For example:

- "The whole purpose of your spiritual path is to let go of and move on from the emotional body. It is the emotional body which the Self hangs on to, holding on to the fear,

Chapter 6: Managing Your Emotions

doubt, jealousy, anger, greed, etc. Often you are not aware that this is happening to you, that the Self is hanging on to these emotions. ... What happens when one releases the emotional body? One sees through the illusion of the Earth plane, one has more energy to give to whatever one wishes to give it to, and one is no longer in anger, greed, fear, jealousy, etc. Because those particular energies are not there, there is more energy to manifest, and more energy to work with on one's spiritual path. ... Once the blocks of the emotional body are removed, the world is yours and so much is possible with the energy you are not using within the emotional body." ~ Maitreya (Newsletter #193, December 11, 2004)

Figure 6-3 illustrates the pattern of emotional states you can expect over time using ***Conscious Living*** principles and techniques.

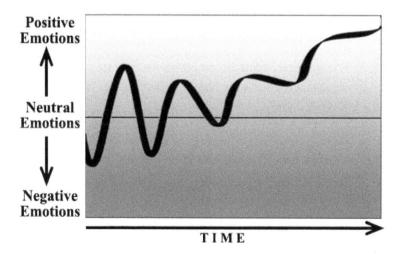

**Figure 6-3
Emotional States in Conscious Living
(Ever-New Joy)**

The term "Ever-New Joy" comes from the Indian master, Paramhansa Yogananda, who described it as <u>knowing</u> *without a doubt* that God, is "ever-existing, ever-conscious, omnipresent, ever-new joy." What he is referring to here is the state of **Alignment** with Higher Self. Similarly, the writings of both Maitreya and Abraham repeatedly refer to the fact that life is meant to be lived in joy. For example:

- "You were born to experience a life with happiness, joy, success, and abundance, but you cannot create that and enjoy that because the Self, like a dog with a bone, keeps chewing away at the negative energy from the past and from unexpressed emotion." ~ Maitreya (Newsletter #69, March 15, 2003)

Note the following keys to understanding the pattern of emotional states in **Conscious Living**.

1. The refinement of emotional states to eliminate the dramatic mood swings characteristic of the 'Roller Coaster' syndrome

2. The gradual elimination of negative emotions *as well as less positive emotions* over time

3. The general trend of emotions over time is increasing degrees of positivity, moving ever closer to a state of 'Ever-New Joy'

In short, a concerted effort toward **Conscious Living** results in progressively less resisting and progressively greater **Allowing** of Source Energy to flow unhindered through the subtle energy bodies as well as through the physical body.

Why are there still fluctuations between less positive and more positive emotional states? The answer is simple. As long as you (as a soul) inhabit a physical body on the earth plane, you will have a SELF trying to pull you down, even if ever so slightly. The Self's sole purpose is to maintain its own existence and its control through fear and doubt. In *Conscious Living*, however, these fluctuations become increasingly smaller. The emotional 'downs' become less frequent and less intense and you experience increasingly more positive emotional 'ups.' This occurs because you gradually begin to 'tame' the Self and live your life progressively less under its influence.

In other words, as you learn to practice *Conscious Living* more frequently and more completely in your daily life, you move out of both the 'Roller Coaster' syndrome and the stilted 'Calm Indifference' patterns toward increasing *Alignment* with Higher Self and the accompanying emotional states of calmness, peacefulness, and 'Ever-New Joy.'

- "The most important decision you make is to be in a good mood." ~ Francois Voltaire (1694–1778, essayist, humanist, rationalist, satirist, and philosopher)

While the linkage between thoughts and emotions sometimes seems unfortunately inescapable, you can use this fact to your advantage in managing your emotions. This is because your emotions directly reflect your vibration at any given point in time. Negative emotions (anger, fear, the name doesn't matter) *always* indicate a conflict between the emotion and what you want in your life. If 'ever-new joy' is a state of *Alignment* with Higher Self, then negative emotions indicate that you are headed in the wrong direction! In other words, you can depend upon *how you feel* to determine if your thoughts (whether or not you are consciously aware of them[B1, C7]) are *Allowing* you to *Align* with Higher Self or causing you to *resist* alignment.

Emotions always mirror subconscious intentions. Whenever there is a discrepancy between (usually) subconscious emotions and conscious intentions, what you *say* you want is inconsistent with what you *feel* you want. Over time, this inevitably leads to trapped energy that needs to be healed.[B2, C6]

Scientific research has repeatedly demonstrated the masterful ability of human beings to *rationalize and distort our thoughts and our perceptions of reality* even in the face of overwhelming evidence to the contrary. This human "ability" (actually dis-ability as recognized by two Nobel Prizes!—Herbert Simon, 1978; Daniel Kahneman, 2002) is used by the Self as an aid to keep us in illusion and in ignorance of the truth. These distortions may help us to 'feel better' in the moment, but will likely become more toxic over time as 'trapped energy.'

Your Vibrational Indicator

Whenever you become aware of an emotional response to ***anything*** (keep in mind that *everything* on the earth plane produces *some* emotional response—positive, neutral, or negative), the *first* thing to do is to **check your Vibrational Indicator** to assess the degree to which you are experiencing **Well-Being or Alignment with Source Energy**. *It's all about the Energy* that you are experiencing and expressing in any given moment.

Recall what I stated back in Chapter 2: "*it is the quality of the emotional vibration—not the words—that really matters.*" The same principle holds for your observations *and* your imagination. The Universe is responding to your vibration regardless of whether you are experiencing something or *just thinking about it* (giving it your attention) *or just imagining it* (again, giving it your attention). The Universe can't tell the difference between the *causes* of your vibration and *the vibration itself. Only the vibration matters.* That is why your vibration is so important. It also greatly simplifies the process of managing your emotions. Your emotions mirror your vibration, and (once again) *you can depend upon how you feel* to determine if your thoughts (whether or not you are consciously aware of them) are ***Allowing*** you to ***Align*** with Higher Self or causing you to *resist alignment.*

Abraham often refers to the "Emotional Guidance System" a 22-step continuum of emotional vibrations (Esther and Jerry Hicks, *Ask and It Is Given*, 2004). It ranges from extremely negative emotions at the bottom (22 = Fear, Grief, Depression, Powerlessness, and Despair) to extremely positive emotions at the top (1 = emotional vibrations of Joy, Knowledge, Empowerment, Freedom, Love, and Appreciation). Why so many levels?

It just isn't possible for most people to make large jumps successfully (for example, from step 15 to step 10—the vibrational difference is just *too big*), and certainly not to maintain such jumps for any significant length of time. Often, trying to move even two or three steps in one leap can cause us to fail. In order to be successful, we need to move up the emotional scale in smaller increments. Hence Abraham's 22-step scale.

Human beings live in the 'comfort zone' where old habits die hard. We are much too conditioned by our families, our experiences (both current and past-life), and our culture to be successful in changing our habits—our way of thinking, our way of feeling, and our way of living—by trying to make *big* changes all at once. Sure, sometimes we make a huge effort to change (especially in the short term). However, we are far more likely to revert back to old ways if we try to make large changes than if we 'incrementalize' our way through change. The old saying,

"Little strokes fell great oaks," is very true when it comes to change. The Self part of us resists change, so making small changes over a longer period of time is far more likely to be successful than attempting large changes undertaken all at once.

Change (discussed in greater detail later[B1, C7; B3, C6] is difficult, often *very* difficult, and substantially improving your emotional state is particularly difficult. Human growth—especially vibrational (emotional) growth—takes time, and large jumps are generally not sustainable. Abraham teaches that moving from a given emotional frequency to a *slightly higher emotional frequency* gradually changes (transforms) your emotional energy field to a higher state, thus making it easier to move up the scale and allowing you to 'habituate' to a higher emotional state before attempting to raise your vibration to the next step.

You might expect the midpoint (11) on Abraham's scale to represent neutral emotions, but it actually represents "Overwhelment"—hardly neutral. In fact, the scale shifts notably off-center from mildly negative emotions (8—Boredom) to mildly positive emotions (7—Contentment). Why is this?

The answer is both simple and actually very useful. It is much more difficult to reach for a higher vibration at the low end of the emotional scale (high numbers) than it is when you are already at a relatively higher level (reflected in a relatively positive emotion—low numbers). Thus, smaller vibrational steps are needed to raise your vibration when your vibration is low. When your vibration is anywhere above neutral, it takes less energy to reach for a higher vibrational step, and success is far more likely. The point is to maximize the likelihood of successfully raising your vibration wherever you find yourself on the scale at any given moment (NOW).

I have chosen *not* to list Abraham's scale here for a very good reason. It is simply an *example* of what a hypothetical personal scale *might* look like at any given point in time. It is not absolute; it is different for different individuals and even for the same individual over time. *It is the <u>emotions</u> (indicators or your vibration) that are important, not the word labels for them.*

The whole point of your checking your *Vibrational Indicator* is to determine where you are (how good/bad do you *feel*?) and then to *reach for a thought that <u>feels a little better</u>* as you move your vibration (as reflected in your feelings, your emotions) up the vibrational scale.

By **reaching for a thought that feels a little bit better using your Emotional Indicator**, you can gradually raise your vibration higher and higher (the ultimate purpose of *Conscious Living*). Thus, *Alignment* with Higher Self—God, Ultimate Being, Source—whatever term you choose, is eventually experienced as an emotional state of profound joy, the top (#1) of Abraham's Emotional Scale. Most importantly, this doesn't have to be a one-time event. The principles and techniques of *Conscious Living* outlined in the **Dancing with the Energy** books can assist you not only to reach, but to *maintain* this level of vibrational *alignment* for increasingly greater proportions of your daily life.

Tips for Working with Your Emotions

T*IP* #1 – C*HECK* Y*OUR* E*MOTIONAL* I*NDICATOR*

Conscious Living involves the conscious and continuous monitoring of your emotions. How can you become more aware of your emotions? There are several very reliable sources of information ranging from constitutional (your general emotional makeup in this lifetime) to energetic and to situational. In order, these are:

- From your Natal Chart[B2, C2]
- Emotions related to pain, dis-ease or physical disease in your body and chakras
- Emotional Triggers[B3, C2], for example:
    - The people close to you.
    - The words others say to you.
    - The situations in which you find yourself.
    - Introspection via journaling, meditation, contemplation, etc.[B3, C4]

If you don't have a label for what you are feeling in any given moment (the NOW), that's okay. *The labels are not important.* If you can, try to give your emotion a number on a 5-point, 10-point, or 100-point scale. Your choice of scale is not important other than that you are comfortable using it. Remember, *what feels better is what serves you better*. It is that simple. Remembering to do it is the hard part, so do it the easy way. Consciously practice it until it becomes a habit, and then you will do it unconsciously in nearly every situation without having to consciously think about it (***Allowing***). That is **Conscious Living.**

TIP #2 – TAKE VIBRATIONAL ACTION FIRST

While intention is critical to accomplishing any task[B1, C5, Tip #3], intention alone is insufficient to achieve anything that you really desire. Some degree of *action* is also required in order for intention to manifest. The problem is that intentions tend to get 'watered down' when we meet with obstacles (including postponing them until the proverbial 'tomorrow'). *Without the discipline of action, intention alone is useless.*

But what, exactly is meant by the term, 'action?' **Action is energy in motion.** Certainly, this refers to *physical action*, but emotions are obviously not physical. So, what does 'taking

Chapter 6: Managing Your Emotions

vibrational action' mean? Abraham-Hicks speaks of **vibrational action as _feeling_ (emotion) and _being_**; the single word, 'action,' is used in the more conventional, physical sense.

The important point here is that you must learn to *take action vibrationally* (emotionally), not just physically with mental activity, words, or bodily effort. Physical action may or may not help you to manifest what you desire, depending on whether it is in **Alignment** (in **Harmony**) *with the vibration of your desire*. Obviously, wishful thinking with no action is not likely to produce results. But physical action *inconsistent with what you are feeling* will not bring you what you want either. You live in a vibrational universe, and the sooner you *use* the laws of that universe to your advantage, the happier and more productive you will be. So, *get your energy lined up first*. This is defined as the 'feeling place' (emotion) of what you desire. Without that, no amount of 'work' (or any other action) will make any difference.

The key here is your **emotions**, what you are **feeling**. They directly reflect your vibrational state, **who you are at the moment**. Whether you like it or not, taking effective action *begins* with your emotions, *followed by* subsequent thoughts, words, and/or deeds. If your thoughts, words, and/or deeds are consistent with those emotions they are more likely to manifest. If they are inconsistent with your emotions, those actions are likely to be ineffective and possibly even counterproductive. So, take action—***vibrational action**—**first*** and then follow it up with harmonizing thoughts, words, and deeds.

Give *almost all* of your attention to your emotional state to get into the *feeling place* of emotional well-being—as close you are able to get yourself to a state of joy. *Then* put the remainder of your effort toward *physical action while maintaining that feeling place*. Think about this strategy (**Balance**): it is about moving forward toward what you desire on the earth plane *and* simultaneously moving ever closer toward *Alignment* with your Higher Self. What more could one want?

TIP #3 – THEN TAKE MENTAL AND/OR PHYSICAL ACTION

In terms of emotions, this means to *Align* your thoughts with Higher Self *after* first *Aligning* your emotions. Remember, you can't successfully *Align* your thoughts with Higher Self all at once. You have to get there gradually by choosing a thought that feels a little better than what you are feeling right NOW. Then, hold that thought; *repeat it over and over until you believe it to be true.*[B3, C3] Repeat your new thought until your *Emotional Indicator* tells you that your emotion NOW has changed (*Allowing*). This may take only a few seconds, a few hours, a few weeks or even a few years, depending on how big a jump you have chosen to make between your old thought and your new thought—*and* the *consistent effort* you put into it. But being overly ambitions about this will get you nowhere fast.

TIP #4 – MANAGE THE FLOW OF EMOTIONAL ENERGY

Let's take a closer look at this notion of emotion as vibrational action. It has been said that "e-motion is energy in motion." And energy that is not in motion becomes stagnant, ineffective, stuck, and even toxic. Maitreya speaks a great deal about 'unused' or stagnant energy to explain this:

- "Everything is energy. Every word that you speak is energy. Every thought you have is energy. Energy has to go somewhere or else it returns to the source. When it returns to the source it has become changed because of the thought that was attached to it. For instance, positive thoughts go

Chapter 6: Managing Your Emotions

out and are used. Positive words that are spoken create more positive energy—they motivate, create, empower. Negative thoughts do one of two things: they either create fear, doubt, insecurity or any other negative emotion, or they go back in and, because they have not been used, they return to their source, negative. Stagnant, unused energy becomes just that—stagnant. Negative words have the same effect." ~ Maitreya (Newsletter #288, February 3, 2010)

Let's briefly examine what Maitreya is saying here. *When energy (emotion) is expressed* (for example, thoughts, words, deeds, etc.), *the vibrations sent out create consequences that resonate with (are in Alignment/Harmony with) the vibrational frequency of that energy.* Thoughts express your desires for something to happen, and specific intentions make those thoughts concrete. Your words give concrete intentions force or impetus and acting on those words facilitates the manifestation of your desires. This is all a function of the basic *Law of Attraction*.

If, however, your thoughts and emotions are *not expressed*, that energy returns to its source (that is, you, the person who 'thought' or 'felt' that energy), again due to the *Law of Attraction*. The energy doesn't just dry up and blow away; it lodges in the soul memory as well as in the etheric and physical bodies as unexpressed, unused, or stagnant energy.[B2, C5; B3, C2] Unexpressed thoughts of what are generally interpreted as positive desires become unfulfilled longing, feelings of disappointment, failure, and low self-esteem. Unexpressed thoughts of what are generally interpreted as negative desires also become lodged in the soul memory as anger, fear, doubt, etc. *Notice that all of these unexpressed thoughts are stored along with their associated <u>emotions</u> (what you are <u>feeling</u>).*

Unused energy is 'stagnant' and becomes 'attached' or 'stuck,' building up pressure within us—much like steam in a pot of boiling water with a tight lid. Just as that steam must eventually be released, stuck energy *must be expressed* at some point. In other words, *unexpressed or stuck energy—regardless of whether you <u>think</u> it is positive or negative—creates a toxic situation that <u>will</u>, sooner or later, come out (be expressed) either in or through your own body (physical, mental, and/or emotional).* The universe, through the inevitable *Law of Attraction*, plays no favorites. It just does what it has to do, which is to *attract to you what you <u>feel</u>; NOT necessarily what you <u>think</u>.*

The important take-away here is the centrality of your emotional state in *everything* that you do. That is why paying conscious attention to your Emotional Indicator is so important. In any given moment, you always have the choice between continuing to feel what you are feeling right NOW or reaching for a thought that feels a little better.

Remember, **stagnant energy is dead energy**. The only thing stagnant energy produces is undesirable consequences (more lessons, more karma, more stuck energy) that **must—and will—eventually be released**, usually at a time and in ways you would rather it didn't, unless you proactively take steps to release and heal or transform it at a time, place, and manner of your choosing.[B2, C5; B3, C2] Energy in motion is free and *can* manifest in more constructive and desirable ways *if* you learn to consciously use that energy in the most effective ways.

Half-hearted emotions, reluctant feelings, etc. are all forms of **resistance**. Similarly, half-hearted actions, reluctant actions, etc. are all forms of **resistance**. Resistance creates dead energy, few if any desired results, and ultimately more lessons to learn. Whatever you decide to do, do it with passion—with conviction—**knowing** that your actions will produce results. Then, whatever physical action you take, do it whole-heartedly, with sincerity, and with no fear or doubt (*Allowing*). I'll discuss ways to reduce and even to eliminate resistance in Books 2 and 3 of *Dancing with the Energy*.

Summary of Tips for Working with Your Emotions

- Tip #1 – Check Your Emotional Indicator
- Tip #2 – Take <u>Vibrational</u> Action <u>First</u>
- Tip #3 – <u>Then</u> Take Mental and/or Physical Action
- Tip #4 – Manage the Flow of Emotional Energy

Conscious Living and Emotions

The process of raising one's vibration is a matter of learning to control the emotional body a greater and greater proportion of each day. This process entails moving out of the 'Roller Coaster syndrome' of unconscious living without muting or stifling the emotions (the 'Calm Indifference' of Stoicism). These modes of emotional living are neither healthy nor natural.

Conscious Living, on the other hand, encourages the healthy expression of emotions. Negative emotions are transformed or replaced with increasingly positive emotional states. This is both the objective and the experience of ***Alignment*** with Higher Self ('Ever-New Joy'). This is the life you are intended to live in its fullest and most abundant form.

Chapter 7: The Conscious and Subconscious Minds

Introduction

We are all well acquainted with the conscious mind. In addition to knowledge learned in this lifetime, it's the emotions we experience and the thoughts we think using our brain—every day, moment-to-moment. We tend to think of the brain as a physical tool used by the body to process sensory inputs (all of which are electro-chemical in nature) from our body's organs (for example, eyes, ears, skin, nose, etc., anywhere on or within the body that has sensory receptors). But it goes far beyond that. *In fact, the brain actually constructs 'memories' of things and events that are consistent with our beliefs even if (objectively) those things never existed or those events never actually occurred.*

We also think of our brains as highly rational, consistent, and efficient information processors but, as of this date, two Nobel Prizes have been awarded (Herbert Simon, 1978; Daniel Kahneman, 2002) on the basis of thoroughly demonstrating the opposite to be the case. Rather than attributing all kinds of potentially inaccurate abilities and characteristics, let's simply say that ***the brain is the physical organ with which we process 'information' (accurate or not, and only some of which we are consciously aware)***.

The information in the conscious mind includes knowledge (for example, 2+2=4, Olympia is the capitol of Washington State, birthdates of family members), as well as the thoughts and emotions of which you are consciously aware. But the conscious mind is quite literally just the "tip of the (proverbial) iceberg" when it comes to consciousness as shown in Figure 7-1. It is everything above the waterline, the Level of Conscious Awareness. Everything below the waterline is the subconscious mind and, much like an iceberg, up to 90% of your consciousness lies below the level of your conscious awareness. While you may be able to glimpse a little bit of an iceberg below the waterline, the details get lost within only a few feet and quickly disappears from sight entirely. Similarly, you may get a glimpse of the subconscious mind from time to time, but its contents remain almost completely unknown until such time as they are triggered[B2, C5] or until you are ready to explore and to deal with them in order to make further progress in becoming the Master of your life and raising your vibration.

Figure 7-1
The Conscious and Subconscious Minds

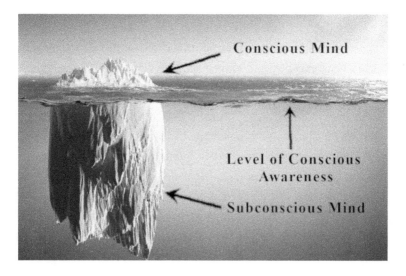

So, what is the 'subconscious mind?' The prefix 'sub' means 'below,' and the word 'conscious' refers to 'awareness.' ***Thus, by definition, the subconscious mind is all the emotions and thoughts that are below the level of conscious awareness, the emotions and thoughts of which we are generally not consciously aware.*** For example, Maitreya writes:

- "You do not realize what is in your subconscious mind deep within your being. Every incarnation you have ever had is in your soul memory. If you have experienced a past life with trauma, sadness, grief, or other emotion and have not released this energy, then it is in this subconscious part of your being." ~ Maitreya (Newsletter #195, February 15, 2007)

- "People think they are calm, yet in sixty percent of the population of the earth, subconscious anger, rage, and frustration lies within the soul. It is hidden and does not manifest itself unless it is triggered. The person, through their lives, holds in all of their frustration; they do not let go of their anger, and it stays inside, accumulating, waiting for the cork to be pulled either in this incarnation or in another." ~ Maitreya (Newsletter #268, December 14, 2009)

Because the subconscious mind is so much deeper and larger than the conscious mind, it plays an incredibly important role in our daily lives; we are just unaware of it until it comes bursting through the surface of our awareness, demanding our attention until we release and heal or transform it. Just think of the sheer magnitude of all the emotions and thoughts we have ever experienced in thousands of past lives, and you begin to see one of the principal reasons why Maitreya says we live 80-85% of our lives in "past-life mode."

As stated in the previous chapter, the Universe cannot distinguish between imagination and 'real' experience; it is all part of the *same* experience in the conscious mind. The same is true of the subconscious mind. In addition, the subconscious mind has no experience of humor; everything is regarded as 'fact' regardless of whether it was either intended or experienced as a 'joke.' Subconscious emotions are 'stored' as vibrations differing only in the intensity to which they felt 'good' or 'bad' at the time they were experienced. Subconscious thoughts are stored as 'fact' based on the vibration of subconscious emotions, whether they have any validity 'in truth' at all.

The contents of the subconscious mind are comprised of energy held in the four 'subtle' or 'energy bodies'[B1, C3] or alternatively, in the Matrix, especially in 'morphic' or 'local fields' of the Matrix.[B1, C4] In essence, *the subconscious mind is the primary repository or storehouse for unexpressed (unused) energy*, meaning that there is some degree of attachment or 'holding on' to the energy. In other words, the trapped energy hasn't yet been cleared or released from your personal energy, your soul, if you will. This trapped energy comes in the form of:

- Life lessons[B2, C3] – Spiritual Energy Field
- Karmic obligations[B2, C4] – Spiritual Energy Field
- Repressed memories from the current life (especially childhood)[B2, C5] – Mental and/or Emotional Energy Fields
- Past-life soul memories[B2, C5] – Mental and/or Emotional Energy Fields
- Unfinished business, meaning anything to which you have an 'attachment'[B2, C5] – Mental and/or Emotional Energy Fields
- Emotions, the fuel of the Self[B1, C6; B2, C5] – Emotional Energy Field, especially
    - Doubts (for example, self-worth/self-esteem issues)
    - Fears and anxieties (for example, being judged by others or oneself, abandonment, spiders, etc.)
- 'Etheric Imprints' of physical conditions or their causes[B2, C3] – Etheric Energy Field

I must add here that *all—everything*—you have ever experienced (thought, felt, said, did) in every lifetime is 'stored' as energetic 'ripples' (vibrations) in the subconscious mind (in the Matrix and in those local fields specific to you—or if you prefer, in your subtle energy fields or energy 'bodies' and the chakras). This includes all the 'good stuff' (love, laughter—any and all positive experiences) in addition to the rather somber and 'negative' contents just listed.

Keep in mind that the list above addresses primarily *unused or trapped energy*. All the 'good stuff' evokes positive emotions because they are *Aligned* with the Higher Self. All the 'bad or negative stuff' comes from **resistance** (*not Allowing* Source energy to flow freely through you), *im-*balance, and *non-alignment* with Higher Self. Remember, you are intended to be living a life of *joy*, not fear, pain, or sorrow. **Conscious Living** is all about learning how to get from 'bad' to 'better, and to better, and to better, and ...,' hence the emphasis on removing resistance and blockages (***Allowing***), learning to ***Balance*** your energies, and steadily moving closer to ever-new joy (***Alignment***).

- "The subconscious mind is an incredible storehouse of emotions and memories—both good and bad—from experiences in this life and from prior lives. Unfortunately, we tend to 'hang on' to negative and traumatic emotions in the soul memory—inadequacy, betrayal, hatred, traumatic death, etc. Unless we release the negative emotions associated with people, places, and events during the lifetime in which they occurred, they become 'trapped' in the soul memory, waiting to come out in this life or in some future lifetime. Because they are so intense and so painful, often they are not released but stay in the background like scripts that we play over and over either consciously or unconsciously. Eventually the energetic pressure from these trapped emotions spills out into the physical body as stress, physical pain, psychological dis-ease and even physical disease." ~ Dennis L. Dossett, PhD ("Emotion Code™ Therapy")

Who cares if 'trapped energy' is in the subconscious mind? So, what? ***Energy is just energy***. It is neither positive nor negative; it just ***is***. But: ***Energy in motion is free and can manifest in constructive, positive ways.*** Unused or unexpressed energy in the subconscious mind is trapped, stagnant, and becomes toxic. Sooner or later it manifests in undesirable ways (for example, physical pain, mental distress. and/or emotional dis-ease, any of which can become the basis for physical and/or emotional disease). When an emotion remains unused or unexpressed (energy with which we identify or to which we are 'attached'), it festers because it is stagnant energy—poisonous energy—and it keeps us from raising our consciousness as well as causing problems in the subtle bodies and eventually in the physical body.

If the energy is not expressed, released, and healed or transformed (remains 'unused'), the only outlet for such energy is the physical body which can suffer from physical pain, disease, and/or emotional pain or dis-ease. Examples of such energy include: anger, frustration, abandonment, fear, doubt, low self-esteem, etc. These topics are discussed later in greater detail.[B2, C5]

Conscious and Subconscious Relationships

Now that you know what is *in* both the conscious and subconscious minds, how are they *related* to each other if at all? You might expect that, if you are consciously aware of one but not the other, any relationship would not be obvious and perhaps would never even be known (let alone understood) by most people. And you would be absolutely correct!

Remember the pattern of emotional states in unconscious living (Figure 6-1)? Why does it look like a roller coaster, wildly bouncing between relatively intense positive and intense negative emotions? Is it all based on unthinking responses to one's external environment? Obviously not, because each of us can think of dozens of people we know personally who share external environments very similar to our own. There has to be something else involved, and there is—the Subconscious Mind, part of one's *internal environment*, which is unique to each individual. No one else shares *exactly* the same soul history as yours. Even if they did, you respond differently to your experiences than other people in the same situations do because of your own (and their) *free will*.

Figure 7-2 shows the relationships between the conscious and subconscious minds in Unconscious Living. Note the wavy dotted line between the conscious mind (top half of the diagram) and the subconscious mind (bottom half). This wavy dotted line represents a kind of 'gray area,' an energetic semi-permeable boundary between them. It is the threshold of awareness. Communication definitely *occurs* between the two minds, but generally we are *aware* of it only occasionally if at all.

Figure 7-2
Relationships Between the Conscious and Subconscious Minds in Unconscious Living

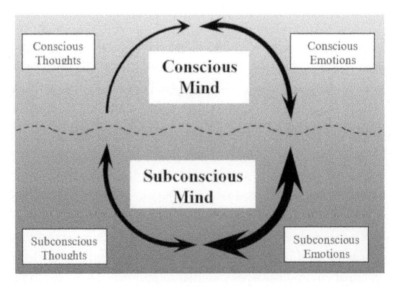

Chapter 7: The Conscious and Subconscious Minds

The conscious mind contains both conscious thoughts[B1, C5] and conscious emotions.[B1, C6] The subconscious mind also contains thoughts (mental body) and emotions (emotional body), but we are generally *not* (or only partially or even vaguely) aware of them. The arrows represent both the direction and the relative strength of a relationship. In other words, thicker arrows indicate a stronger influence than thinner arrows.

Figure 7-2 shows that, in Unconscious Living, your conscious emotions generally influence your conscious thoughts to a far greater extent than vice versa. This reflects some of the systematic biases and distortions so prevalent in human decision making (yes, those same two Nobel Prizes referenced earlier! — Herbert Simon, 1978, and Daniel Kahneman, 2002). Combined with the erratic emotional states (the 'Roller Coaster' effect) so prevalent in mass consciousness, it is little wonder that human information processing and behavior is often irrational and unproductive at worst and very often not optimal even when we are at our mental and emotional 'best.'

Figure 7-2 also shows that subconscious emotions have a much greater effect on both conscious emotions and subconscious thoughts than the reverse. In other words, the subconscious mind is a far more powerful contributor to your daily experience of life than are the contents of the conscious mind.

Note that Figure 7-2 shows no arrowhead (indicating direct influence) leading from conscious thoughts to subconscious thoughts. Thus, the influence of conscious thoughts on subconscious thoughts is *indirect*, largely routed through and driven by conscious and subconscious emotions. The implications of this are not very helpful in terms of 'rational' (for example, thought or 'talk' therapy) approaches to changing deep-seated subconscious thoughts. However, there are other therapeutic strategies[B2, C5] that deal specifically with the subconscious emotional barriers to changing subconscious thoughts.

Let's contrast the Unconscious Living scenario with what happens in *Conscious Living* shown in Figure 7-3. In *Conscious Living*, one's conscious thoughts generally have a greater influence on conscious emotions than vice versa. This is necessary in order for your ***conscious thoughts to create your reality rather than your emotions creating your reality***. It is also clear that both subconscious thoughts and subconscious emotions have relatively little effect on either conscious thoughts or conscious emotions. This reflects what will subsequently be discussed as the process of 'non-attachment' (not to be confused with the Stoic's 'Calm Indifference' in Figure 6-2).

Figure 7-3
Relationship Between the Conscious
and Subconscious Minds in Conscious Living

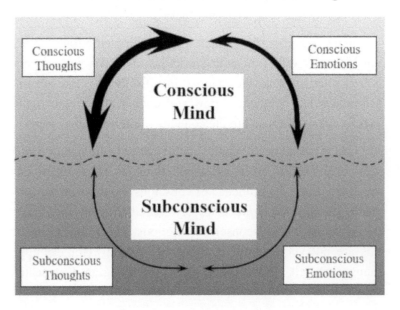

- "The true *balance* of spirituality on the earth plane is to have no emotional body." ~ Maitreya (Newsletter #131, October 29, 2004)

- "You and you alone are the creator of what you want in your life. You can create abundance or lack. However, if you have much deep subconscious patterning from the past, it needs to be removed before you can move forward." ~ Maitreya (Newsletter #223, March 2, 2009)

And what is the overall effect of *Conscious Living*? *Allowing* your energies to flow freely, *Balancing* your energies, and *Aligning* with your Higher Self.

"When you start to deal with what is deep within you, gradually you find more and more peace! As you do this, the body begins to respond to the Higher Self, and this energy will begin to dictate what you need and what you do not need. You will resonate with what it tells you. You will no longer have the cravings you used to have, for they are connected to the emotional part of you. As you raise the vibration, deal with your blocks—release them—you lose more and more of the emotional body! Your higher Self then has control. You will feel so different when this occurs." ~ Maitreya (Newsletter #97, February 10, 2004)

Dealing with Unexpressed or Unused Energy

So how do people typically deal with this unexpressed or unused energy? They are not consciously aware of it until it is 'triggered' by some person or event, and the pent-up emotions from the past come boiling up to the surface—often violently. Why are people 'attached' to this energy? Why are they holding on to it and haven't yet allowed it to be cleared or released? There are two major mechanisms widely researched and accepted in the fields of psychology and counseling relevant to this issue: Repression and Denial.

Repression occurs when one finds a negative emotion so unpleasant or distasteful that they (typically unconsciously) block it from their conscious awareness, preventing what IS from even being recognized as existing. Repression is self-defeating and only prolongs the pain and suffering. The individual 'detaches' from the emotion in the sense that the negative emotion *doesn't consciously exist* for them, but it still resides in the *subconscious mind*. This occurs because of:

- Conditioning (for example, "it's not 'nice' to think or talk about such things")
- It is too scary to deal with (for example, "it's too traumatic to think about" or "it's out of my comfort zone")
- One doesn't know how to deal with it (for example, "I'm at a total loss as to what to do, so I won't think about it just now")

Denial occurs when one recognizes the existence of a negative emotion but rejects it as untrue despite what may be overwhelming evidence to the contrary. Denial is also self-defeating and only prolongs the pain and suffering. Denial is more comfortable than facing what IS, and the individual 'detaches' from the emotion in the sense that the negative emotion is *disavowed or rejected* but it still resides in the *subconscious mind*. This occurs because of:

- Fears and anxieties (for example, "I'm OK," "it's not relevant," etc.)
- Value issues (for example, low self-worth or self-esteem)

Chapter 7: The Conscious and Subconscious Minds

- Feeling one is being judged by others (for example, blame) or by oneself (for example, guilt)

In short, in denial one refuses to accept (let alone recognize) the 'objective truth' (if there is such a thing!) regardless of any evidence to the contrary.

- "Denial is a belief that comes from the beliefs of others, from their own hang-ups and suppressions, their own fears and beliefs. One cannot have *Balance* with denial." ~ Maitreya (Newsletter # 111, June 10, 2004)

While the psychological mechanisms of repression and denial are typical reactions for the mass of humanity, they are not effective—indeed, they are quite destructive in the long run. In **Conscious Living**, however, one begins to understand these reactions and to take positive steps toward dealing with unexpressed or unused energy. This involves the clearing or healing of these energies.

Clearing or Healing Subconscious Emotions is essentially a process of detaching from them. An emotion is a feeling associated with a belief (a thought) with which we identify or to which we are attached. When we deny it, it is still held in the emotional body, and when we repress it or bottle it up, it gets 'stuck' in the emotional body. Our beliefs and emotions have a specific 'energy signature' (colored by our own experience in the context of previous—often past-life—experiences) that makes them unique to us (think local fields in the Matrix). As noted previously, if the energy is not expressed or released (that is, remains 'unused'), the only outlet is the physical body which will eventually suffer from physical pain, disease, and/or emotional pain or dis-ease. I will discuss the healing and release of subconscious emotions later.[B2, C5; B3, C1, C2]

133

Note that I am speaking here of *detach<u>ing</u>* (letting it go) and *not* about becoming *detach<u>ed</u>*. *Detach<u>ment</u>* literally means 'indifference to worldly concerns: aloofness.' Both repression and denial are forms of 'detachment' and they are not helpful.

When Maitreya says (as he so often does) "Give it no energy," he is referring specifically to 'letting go.' The end product of letting go (detaching) is <u>not</u> detachment, it is *non-attachment*. *Non-attachment is the end result of the process of healing (detaching) and is <u>necessary for progress</u> in soul growth as well as every positive aspect of life (spiritual, mental, emotional, and physical) on the earth plane.*

The essence of nonattachment is 'letting go' of anything and everything that does not serve you. Detachment (or being detached) from negative emotions is only covering them up; *it is <u>not</u> healing them. Detach<u>ment</u> is not good.* Detach*ing* from any part of life to the point of becoming detached is allowing your Self to gain control of an otherwise positive process. Detach*<u>ment</u>* is a seriously imbalanced end result and only strengthens trapped energy. Detachment only prolongs the suffering and holds you back.

When you are detached (not acknowledging it, bottling it up, not <u>letting</u> go), you are constantly on guard on a subconscious level and you cannot live life to the fullest. But you are on this earth plane to **engage fully with life**, to maximize your opportunities to learn to become a better version of yourself. That can only happen when the trapped energy is not only released, but is actually either **healed or transformed** (non-attachment). Only then can all your life energies flow freely to bring **Balance** among them and, consequently, **Alignment** with Higher Self. Only then can you truly *en*-joy life, that is, infuse your life with the joy that every one of my wisest teachers says is your birthright.

Chapter 7: The Conscious and Subconscious Minds

In short, the battle (indeed the war) between the Self and the Higher Self is all about **non-attachment, <u>not</u> detachment.** There is a tremendous difference between them, and the sooner one recognizes that fact and acts on it, the sooner they will be able to progress in *all* areas of life.

Tips for Dealing with Subconscious Emotions

The following Tips for dealing with subconscious emotions are similar to those for dealing with conscious emotions.[B1, C6] They are, after all, emotions! However, there are some particular aspects that are unique to subconscious emotions.

TIP #1 – CHECK YOUR EMOTIONAL INDICATOR

How can you become consciously aware of what is in the subconscious mind? The key is to use your **Emotional Indicator** to assess how you *feel.* Emotions are all about feelings, but you are not always consciously aware of *why* you feel the way you do at any given moment (**Balance**). When you are not consciously sure of *why* you feel that way, you can be pretty sure you are dealing with a *subconscious emotion*.

TIP #2 – ACCEPT YOUR SUBCONSCIOUS EMOTIONS

It is much easier to accept emotions of which you are consciously aware, especially if you also have some understanding of where they originated and why. However, subconscious emotions tend to 'boil up' when you least expect it, sometimes quite violently. You often can't put a clear or precise label on them, you generally don't understand *where* they came from, and most importantly, you generally have no clue about *why* you are experiencing them. All you generally know for sure is that they *feel real* and often quite *intense*. Accept what *IS*. *Actively acknowledge* what you are feeling without judgment, resistance, denial, or repression. *Allow yourself to embrace your emotions without fear and without guilt.* It is important to *consciously accept what IS* and then take conscious steps to deal with what you are feeling.

- "It is your *resistance to what is* that causes your suffering." ~ Gautama Buddha

Tip #3 – Understand Your Subconscious Emotions

The next step is to *continually monitor how you are feeling* over a period of time (for example, several hours, days, even weeks). By continually monitoring how you feel and what you are thinking about at the time, you may begin to develop an understanding of where your feelings originate (*Balance*). And of course, there are additional resources that may help you to identify the nature and source of your subconscious emotions:

- From your Natal Chart[B2, C2]
- Emotions related to pain or disease in your body and imbalanced chakras[B2, C5]
- Emotional Triggers[B3, C2], for example:
- The people close to you
- The words others say to you
- The situations in which you find yourself

During this period of monitoring your emotions, introspection through journaling, meditation, and/or contemplation can be invaluable in providing clues to the origin of your subconscious feelings.[B3, C4] You may even become aware of past-life energy (through regression or other procedures) that needs to be cleared[B2, C5] in order to identify where your feelings originate.

Tip #4 – Formulate a Conscious Intention

Changing your identification with or attachment to an emotion is a <u>choice</u>. Conscious Intention + action leads to non-attachment—completely letting go. True non-attachment requires understanding the 'what and why' of your emotions and accepting the responsibility for your own soul evolution. This often means getting out of the comfort zone. Regardless of the source of your emotions, choose to detach from them, especially *negative emotions and emotional swings.* Non-attachment from your emotions (***Allowing***) is necessary in order to free yourself to be *YOU*, to become the *Master of your life and to raise your level of consciousness.*

Tip #5 – Detach from Your Subconscious Emotions

Taking action to clear your subconscious emotions (***Allowing***) is extremely important. *Passive acceptance is often accompanied by conscious intention, but <u>without</u> action.* Some people recognize and accept their negative emotions, but choose to wallow in them. This involves staying in the comfort zone, taking the easy way out, and usually results only in blaming other people and/or playing the 'victim.' It is self-defeating and only prolongs the emotional (and sometimes physical) pain and suffering. In essence, staying in the comfort zone means that success can only come by accident rather than through your conscious efforts. **Conscious Living** is far more likely to bring you the quality of life you desire as well as raising your vibration, the opportunities for soul growth you intended to capitalize on when you incarnated into your current life.

When you are bothered by emotions, conscious or subconscious, you are dealing with trapped or unused energy. Follow through on your conscious intention to detach from trapped energy by taking steps to clear it from your energy fields. Releasing or clearing trapped energy is a continuous process, and generally doesn't happen all at once. Typically, clearing will occur in stages as you are 'vibrationally *ready*' or capable of doing so.

Completely clearing or healing trapped energy may take anywhere from a few hours to several years, depending on the intensity of the emotion and the degree of trauma involved when it was created. It is also dependent on your '*vibrational readiness*' to deal with it. The higher your vibration, the deeper the clearing process. After all, the Universe is really trying to help you to raise your vibration as much as possible, but only as quickly and as completely as you are vibrationally ready for it. Clearing can be a slow and sometimes painful process but it does get better. Again, the higher your initial vibration, the faster and more complete your efforts to clear trapped emotions will be.

I will briefly discuss some tools you can use to help clear trapped emotions in "Releasing Past-life Energy"[B2, C5] and in "Health, Well-Being and Energy Healing"[B3, C2], as well as under the topic of reprogramming the subconscious mind.[B3; C3, C5] These can be an extremely important part of your clearing process.

Habits and the Subconscious Mind

Habits are part of the subconscious mind because they are generally below the level of conscious awareness unless they are triggered by the realization that they are either inappropriate or are not serving you well in a particular situation. At that point you may (or may not) be motivated to consciously think and act in a different manner. However, because they are generally not invested with intense emotional energy, they are different from the trapped or unused energies discussed previously in this chapter.

So, what is meant by the term 'habit?' First, *a habit is a learned behavior* you have come to rely on to make life simpler or easier to deal with cognitively. The human brain is a marvelous creation, but it does not have unlimited capabilities. In fact, research by psychologists, economists, and marketers shows quite clearly that human beings are relatively limited information processors (thinkers). This is especially true when (a) there is a large amount of information, (b) the information is relatively complex, and (c) when one's ego (particularly self-esteem) is involved. Under these circumstances people tend to invoke two basic rules: (1) Simplify and (2) Feel good. In other words, as information processors we humans are pretty good at much of what we do, but what we do is quite often not very good!

Habits are very helpful to us when the task is relatively simple, repetitive, and when the consequences of error are relatively minor. In such situations, habits can be very convenient and efficient ways of responding to our environment. For example: A long time ago I learned how to tie my shoelaces. It is a relatively simple task (it doesn't require much in the way of mental resources), I do it at least once a day, and if I mess up and get a knot in my shoelace it really isn't a big deal. I rely on this habit a lot and I'm personally glad that I do. I don't really want to spend much time or mental energy thinking about how to tie my shoelaces!

However, ***habits can be very detrimental*** when (a) the task is relatively complex (it requires a great deal of mental resources and constant adaptive changes in behavior), (b) the task is performed infrequently, and (c) when the consequences of error are potentially quite severe. In such situations, the brain often gets overloaded. For example: Several years ago, a technician in an electrical distribution company in the American state of New Mexico was replacing a component of the electrical power grid as part of periodic maintenance. The task wasn't especially difficult but did require many very specific steps, and he hadn't done it very many times previously. He didn't notice a critical nuance that was different about this particular component and followed the steps that he had relied on in previous similar situations (habit). This resulted in his making an error which shut down the entire electrical power grid for much of Arizona, New Mexico, and southern California for several hours. He didn't even realize that he was responsible for the loss of power until several hours later.

The point here is that ***a habit is an <u>unconscious</u> behavior***. It is generally not a part of our conscious awareness until something unusual happens to draw our active attention to it.

Where do habits come from? As stated previously, they are ***learned through prior experience***, much of it in the present lifetime through culture, family, social influences, religion, beliefs, etc. Such habits are a form of ***conditioning*** useful for survival and coping with life. These conditioned habits become part of your self-identity (Ego, who you think you are) without your realizing it. Habitual conditioned beliefs in particular can hold you back from changing your situation, raising your consciousness, and becoming the Master of your life.

However, *many habits originate in the subconscious mind rather than being learned*—they often stem from the emotional energy of fear and doubt from past lives trapped in the soul memory. In addition, many of our personal characteristics are holdovers from past-life energy, including our talents, aptitudes, and even some of our personality traits.

- Where do your habits come from? Why do you do the things you do? I will tell you why; it is the combination of your past life memories and your chosen star pattern for this incarnation. Each soul chooses a life path, and that life path is influenced by the movements of the planets, asteroids and stars in their lifetime. It is this which brings out what is needed for you to clear away habits, some of which have been in a particular soul memory for many incarnations. The fears you have are also triggered by these planets. It is the movement of the planets and asteroids which assist you to deal with these. Along with your desire to do so, you can successfully remove many blocks, fears and many emotions if you look to the pattern of the planets and asteroids in your life. ~ Maitreya (Newsletter #16, June 21, 2001)

Talent or Aptitude refers to the inborn capacity to perform certain tasks (for example, compose or perform music, draw or paint, design and/or fix equipment and machinery (cars, refrigerators, orbiting space laboratories, etc.). So-called 'child prodigies' who exhibit extraordinary talent at an early age are frequent examples of souls who have mastered those skills in other lifetimes (old habits). Other people are sometimes referred to as 'a natural' when performing certain tasks. They are often simply repeating well-practiced behaviors learned in a previous lifetime.

While there is scientific evidence that some personality traits may have a small genetic component[B3, C1], the bulk of their origin is attributed to learning/conditioning from the environment early in a person's life. What scientists don't realize is that an individual's personality traits are often 'leftover' or 'trapped' energies from prior lifetimes.

When an individual consistently displays behaviors that are not obviously caused by their environment, other people tend to attribute their behavior to personality traits such as angry, moody, withdrawn, confident, nurturing, rigid, carefree, judgmental, playing the 'victim,' etc. How often have you heard statements such as "That's the way he is *wired*," or "He was *born* that way"? The key is that those behaviors often were well-practiced habits accompanying emotionally-laden events (trapped energy) that occurred long before the individual incarnated into their current life.[B2, C5]

- "Our deeds still travel with us from afar,
  And what we have been makes us what we are."
  ~ George Eliot (1819–1880; novelist, poet, journalist; *Middlemarch*, 1872)

In any case, your major personality characteristics and aptitudes are **reflected in your astrological natal chart**.[B2, C2] For example, astrological signs are classified as cardinal, fixed, or mutable. Fixed signs in particular tend to have strong habits and more judgment, rigidity, etc. carried over into the present lifetime.

Habits reflect your 'comfort zone' precisely because you don't have to give them much conscious attention and because they are so easy to perform. The comfort zone is always the 'easy way out' of responding to anything or anyone in your environment. Consequently, habits are one of the chief causes of getting 'stuck' on the spiritual path because you stop growing in the comfort zone; change is avoided as long as the pain of continuing what you are accustomed to doing is less than the pain of stepping out of the comfort zone into a new way of 'doing' (including habits). Suffering from something that is familiar is generally preferred over fear of the unknown. Thus, habits are a major tool used by the Self to keep you from raising your consciousness and becoming the master of your life.

Tips for Changing Your Habits

Changing a habit is essentially a _process_ of detaching from the habit. Some of the steps are similar to those for dealing with subconscious emotions, but there are some differences as well. Changing a habit is generally not a quick and easy process; it involves several requirements in order to be successful. It is likely to take a good deal of conscious effort over a period (often extended period) of time.

- "Habit is habit, and not to be flung out of the window by any man, but coaxed down-stairs a step at a time." ~ Mark Twain (*Pudd'nhead Wilson*, 1894)

TIP #1 – BRING YOUR HABITS TO CONSCIOUS AWARENESS

The first requirement is **conscious awareness** of the habit. Whether the habit involves your thoughts, attitudes, personality characteristics, behaviors, or some combination of these, you can't really do anything about them unless you recognize that they are part of who you *currently* are. This is a matter of *acknowledging* your habits, the first requirement in the change process (***Allowing***).

Tip #2 – Consciously Accept Your Habits

Second, whether or not you like or approve of your habits (judgment), you need to ***consciously accept*** what ***is***. Human beings ***are*** creatures of habit by nature, and simply repressing your habits or denying their existence will get you nowhere fast in changing them. Both repression and denial are subtle and easy ways used by the Self to resist change by *not allowing* your energies to flow naturally.

Essentially, 'fighting' your habits only results in giving them more attention and making them more powerful influences on your life. By *accepting them* (***Allowing***), you strip them of power over your life and you can begin to deal with them more constructively.

Tip #3 – Understand Your Habits

Third, in order to avoid resisting the acknowledgment of a habit, you need to examine your conditioned beliefs and fears regarding what is 'acceptable' behavior (***Balance***). Habits based on conditioning and/or fear stop the natural flow of energy (*not allowing)*. They sabotage your acceptance of change, the raising of your consciousness, and becoming your own Master.

Understanding a habit begins with understanding your underlying beliefs and feelings. What are your conscious and subconscious fears? What lessons[B2, C3] did you intend to learn in this incarnation? What karma[B2, C4] did you intend to **Balance** in this lifetime? What past-life issues[B2, C5] are you carrying forward into this lifetime? Genuinely understanding the ego/Self helps

Chapter 7: The Conscious and Subconscious Minds

you to fully acknowledge your habits and to make better choices about how to change them. For example, if you have the habit of complaining about the attitudes or behavior of others, the Universe is simply telling you what you need to know about yourself (mirroring).

Sometimes, a self-defense mechanism kicks in and we 'play the victim,' often blaming others for our own habits. And, indeed, we are not always alone in our resistance. The Self is notorious for enlisting resistance from others who often reinforce our subconscious doubts and fears. Social pressures from family, friends, peers, and society are part of the 'comfort zone' that holds us back as previously discussed.

Simply 'renouncing' your habits is only another form of 'fighting' them, and it doesn't work. Giving them more attention only ties you to them more strongly than before. Working to *understand* your habits, however, helps you to 'see through' the illusion that they are helpful and deserve an 'honored place' in your life not only as 'who you are', but more importantly as 'who you *want to be.*' When viewed in this fashion, understanding the true value of a habit eventually leads to simply dropping it because it doesn't serve you anymore. It is much easier in the long run and actually provides the most effective solution to the problem of changing your habits.

Tip #4 – Consciously Intend to Change One Habit

The fourth requirement in successfully changing habits is *conscious intention (Alignment). Habits don't change by accident; they change by choice.* The conscious intention to change is often much more difficult to accomplish than actually changing the habit itself. This is because the Self understands that conscious intention to change is the beginning of getting out of the comfort zone, moving ahead despite its efforts to keep you there. Consequently, you can expect the conscious decision to change a habit will bring out the Lower Self's 'big guns,' fear and doubt.

Note that Tip #4 refers to a *single* habit. *Don't* try to change a number of habits all at once—unless you really want to fail. I don't even recommend prioritizing what you want to change and then start with the most important one (which is likely to be the biggest change in your list!). Why? Earlier in this chapter when I introduced Abraham's "Emotional Guidance System," I noted that it just isn't possible for most people to make large 'jumps' (that is, *changes*) successfully—the vibrational difference is just *too big*. There are two old sayings that are useful to keep in mind: "Little strokes fell great oaks," and "Little steps for little feet." *'Little' or 'small' is much easier to deal with than 'huge' or 'overwhelming' and is <u>always</u> more than 'nothing.'*

I recommend following both Tip #3 from Chapter 5 (State Your Intention Clearly) as well as the scientific evidence supporting the use of effective performance goals. As a review, such goals should be:

- *Specific* (quantifiable) vs. general (for example, 'do your best')
- *Difficult* but attainable
- *Accepted* by the performer

Everything we know about habits tells us they are very difficult to change, so don't worry too much about trying to set an extremely difficult goal. Rather, set your intention to change a habit (behavior) that you *know* you can change successfully with a moderate amount of effort. Then follow each of the remaining

Chapter 7: The Conscious and Subconscious Minds

Tips for changing habits below. When you work on one habit (not too large a change) at a time, success is far more likely. When that habit has been successfully replaced with a better habit (see below), celebrate your success and then begin the cycle of "Tips for Changing Your Habits" (this chapter) again.

TIP #5 – CHANGE YOUR THOUGHTS FIRST

The reason for working with your thoughts[B1, C5] *before* trying to change your emotions is simple. **Habits are learned behaviors**, so changing habits must first take into account changing *conscious* thoughts and feelings (***Alignment***). If you don't work to change the cause of behaviors, you can't realistically expect success in trying to change them.

- "Sow a thought and you reap an action; sow an act and you reap a habit; sow a habit and you reap a character; sow a character and you reap a destiny." ~ Ralph Waldo Emerson

Chapter 5 provided Tips for using your thoughts effectively. But how can you work to ***change both your conscious and subconscious thoughts***? While the material in Chapter 5 is very useful in this regard, I have devoted an especially helpful chapter ("Making Your Affirmations Work!"[B3, C3]) to that topic.

TIP #6 – CHANGE YOUR BEHAVIOR (HABIT)

<u>Don't</u> *try to <u>stop</u> the old behavior (habit); <u>replace</u> it with a <u>better</u> behavior (habit).* As noted earlier, renouncing a habit only makes it stronger because you are giving your attention (energy) to it. It is much easier and more effective to take action by replacing an old habit with a new, better habit (***Alignment***)— *even if it isn't as 'good' as the habit you ultimately want to have. Perform the action or behavior repeatedly until it sticks.* Use

147

'*affirmations that work*'[B3, C3] to help cement your thoughts and emotions during the process. Remember, changing habits is a *process*—sometimes a lengthy and frustrating one—but necessary in order to raise your vibration.[B3, C6]

- "Excellence is an art won by training and habituation. We do not act rightly because we have virtue or excellence, but rather we have those because we have acted rightly. We are what we repeatedly do. Excellence, then, is not an act but a habit." ~ Aristotle (384–322 BCE; Greek critic, philosopher, physicist, and zoologist)

Summary of Tips for Conscious & Subconscious Minds

TIPS FOR DEALING WITH SUBCONSCIOUS EMOTIONS

- Tip #1 – Check Your Emotional Indicator
- Tip #2 – Accept Your Subconscious Emotions
- Tip #3 – Understand Your Subconscious Emotions
- Tip #4 – Formulate a Conscious Intention
- Tip #5 – Detach from Your Subconscious Emotions

TIPS FOR CHANGING YOUR HABITS

- Tip #1 – Bring Your Habits to Conscious Awareness
- Tip #2 – Consciously Accept Your Habits
- Tip #3 – Understand Your Habits
- Tip #4 – Consciously Intend to Change <u>One</u> Habit
- Tip #5 – Change Your Thoughts FIRST
- Tip #6 – Change Your Behavior (Habit)

Conscious Living and the Subconscious Mind

Everything discussed in this chapter lies at the heart of **Conscious Living**, and will be discussed later from a different perspective.[B2, C1] To a great extent, **Conscious Living** involves learning about and working with the subconscious mind to *Allow* your energies to flow freely in order to *Balance* those energies for the purpose of *Aligning* them with your Higher Self.

Chapter 8: Understanding Conscious Living

Introduction

Each book in the entire series of *Dancing with the Energy* books deals with the concept of **Conscious Living**. To this point in Book 1, the chapters have examined the *Foundations of Conscious Living*, but that concept has not really been defined as yet. What do I mean by **Conscious Living**? Well, let's begin by first talking about what I mean by *Unconscious Living*.

Unconscious Living

To put it simply, **Unconscious Living is based on conditioning, programming, and habit.** This is the primary way that the greatest proportion of people live most (if not all) of their lives. It is certainly the type of living associated with **Mass or Base Consciousness**[B1, C1], but it is also characteristic of many people who would say they are 'on the path' and (at least *say* they) consciously desire to raise their consciousness. **Unconscious living** is characterized by:

- Staying in the comfort zone, resisting change, clinging to the old and familiar, clinging to family, friends, and relationships for no better reason than to avoid facing your fears and taking responsibility for your own health, happiness, and abundance.

- Going along with the crowd, trying to fit in, and being a 'good sheep' in the flock; complying with other people's expectations and demands on you and your behavior in order to keep peace, whether you agree with them or not.

- Living much of the time in fear, doubt, and insecurity—in other words, under the totalitarian rule of the Self and the Ego—rather than striving to become the Master of your life and truly raising your consciousness.

In short, unconscious living is characteristic of the earlier stages of soul evolution (for example, 'mass consciousness') but is, unfortunately, routinely found among those who have already attained higher levels of consciousness.[B1, C1] Such individuals often complain of being 'stuck' or 'plateaued'—not making the progress in soul evolution they desire or expect. Unconscious Living is the primary culprit they face.

Conscious Living

Conscious Living, in contrast, is all about '*me*' taking responsibility for learning *my* life lessons, balancing *my* karmic energy, and detaching from *my* trapped energy. It is about me taking responsibility for *my* happiness and *my* decisions about living *my* life. Things don't just 'happen' in my life, ***I create or attract them***. This is the message of the Ancient Wisdoms and the human experience all the way up to and including quantum physics. But this very fact places the power to create the life that 'I' (*YOU*) desire directly into *your own* hands.

Conscious Living is a way to take conscious control of your life with the purpose of raising your level of consciousness and living each day with increasing levels of ever-new-joy.[B1, C6] Its objective is ***Alignment*** of one's energies with Higher Self through ***Balancing*** the energies of life and ***Allowing*** them systematically to flow unhindered—without resistance—through your physical, emotional, mental, and spiritual life.

Conscious Living is accomplished by implementing specific steps for practical application—moment-to-moment—in your daily life. These steps are delineated not only in this chapter, but also in nearly every chapter of the *Dancing with the Energy* books as they relate to ***Conscious Living***. In general, there are three primary components including awareness, choice, and non-judgment.

General Tips for Creating Conscious Living

Tip #1 – Refine Your Awareness of Every Situation

This means becoming aware of what is going on in your life without being trapped or victimized by it. It involves recognizing and acknowledging both the 'good' parts and the 'bad' parts of your life as the simple facts regarding ***what IS***—without resistance. It also includes working to positively deal with the 'bad' parts, a major component of which is ***detaching from negative emotions—Allowing***.[B1, C6] Awareness includes:

- *Awareness of what you think*—your thoughts really do create your reality and your beliefs are your thoughts on steroids; they are your current truth.[B1, C5]

- *Awareness of your subconscious thoughts and emotions*, especially unexpressed/unused energies.[B1, C7]

- *Awareness of what you speak*—speaking your thoughts aloud gives them more power for good *or* ill.[B3, C3]

- *Awareness of what others are mirroring <u>for you</u>*. Note the emphasis on *'<u>for</u> you'* as opposed to *'<u>to</u> you.'* We generally don't like it when other people mirror for us, but they are actually doing us a great favor whether we (or they) know it. They are simply showing us what is inside of ourselves. *We choose* whether to consciously acknowledge it, accept it, and work with it—or not.

TIP #2 – TAKE RESPONSIBILITY FOR YOUR CHOICES

You not only have the <u>right</u> *to choose*, but in **Conscious Living** you also consciously accept the fact that you have the <u>responsibility</u> *to* <u>consciously</u> <u>choose</u> *everything you experience in your life* (***Allowing***). You and every other soul made a number of choices before incarnating into this life, all reflected in the astrological configuration you chose to implement at the time of birth.[B2, C2] These are the broad patterns of challenges and opportunities facing you in your current life. Other choices you make day-by-day, moment-by-moment. ***Conscious Living*** means that you are aware of all of this and accept the responsibility for making *all* of these choices. Before you incarnated, *YOU* (your Higher Self)*:*

- *chose* the *lessons* (non-obligatory unbalanced energy) you wanted to work on in this life and you *choose* whether to face your fears or to run away from each lesson.[B2, C3]
- *chose* what *karma* (unbalanced energy obligations) to try to resolve and you *choose* whether to stand and face such situations in this life or run away from them.[B2, C4]
- *chose* the *past-life energy* you wanted to release in this incarnation and you *choose* whether to follow through with that intention or whether to keep it bottled up in the subconscious mind until later in this or in a future incarnation.[B2, C5]

Intention in your choices is critical.[B1, C5] However, your spoken words sometimes do not accurately reflect the thoughts underlying your choices. Actual behavior is the most accurate indicator of the true intention underlying anyone's choices (*Alignment*). For example, when you tell the Universe that you intend to become your own master and raise your consciousness but then make choices about your behavior based on fear, doubt, insecurity, or the comfort zone, the <u>real</u> *intention* behind those choices is revealed as the naked witness to the truth. But even that is your choice! Just be aware of that fact and take responsibility for it. You are not expected to be perfect! *Allow* yourself (and others) a little leeway here. "<u>Progress</u> *is our most important product!*"

TIP #3 – AVOID JUDGING YOURSELF AND OTHERS

Initially, *non-judgment* (*Alignment* and *Allowing*) brings you the opportunity to grow into unconditional love and, through practice, eventually brings the capacity for exercising it. However, <u>learning</u> *non-judgment is necessary for opening your heart chakra*[B2, C1] *and raising your consciousness.* This is tough to accomplish but, with practice, it can be done. To paraphrase Shakespeare's *Hamlet*: "To judge or not to judge, that is the question!" Moment-to-moment, every day, it is your choice!

Chapter 7 presented tips for "Work[ing] to Understand Your Subconscious Emotions" and "Work[ing] to Understand Your Habits." The point of those tips is to increase awareness— ***observation without judgment***. Judgment *stops* any attempt to understand regardless of the topic.

People often intuitively understand that judging others is not helpful on the spiritual path, but not judging oneself? Shouldn't we always be on the lookout for our own human and spiritual failures and strive to correct them? Why should we not be critical judges of ourselves?

The answer is simple: ***self-examination is* a *process while judgment is but one end result of that process***—and a very negative one at that. ***Conscious Living*** is all about self-examination and then taking conscious steps to raise your level of consciousness (a positive result). However, judgment is almost always negative and immediately stops the natural flow of your life energies (***not allowing***, or resistance). There is no useful purpose for judgment except that used by the Self to stop the progress of your soul evolution dead in its tracks.[B1, C1]

There are four additional Tips for Conscious Living that deal directly with consciously managing your emotional state and consequently your vibration at any given moment.[B1, C6] I will list them again here for your convenience. They are important components of ***Conscious Living*** because they apply to *every* situation:

Tip # 4 – Check your Emotional Indicator

Make it a habit periodically throughout your day to stop what you are doing/thinking for a moment to **assess how you are feeling** (**Alignment** and **Allowing**) right NOW.[B1, C6, C7] Then proceed with further steps to **feel a little better in the present moment.**

Tip # 5 – Choose a Thought That Feels a Little Better

The only guaranteed way to raise your vibrational level right NOW is to consciously take command of your thoughts by focusing them on something that **feels a little better** than what you are feeling right NOW (**Alignment**).[B1, C6]

Tip # 6 – Take <u>Vibrational</u> Action <u>First</u>

Intention without **vibrational action** will likely produce nothing of value or benefit to your life because your energies are *not balanced*. First, focus on your **feelings** in order to attune (**align**) that energy with your conscious intentions. This will automatically help to **balance** your energies. **Balance** is necessary for complete **Alignment**, but first getting your feelings lined up with your intentions (**alignment**) will automatically shift any situation toward greater **balance**.[B1, C6]

Tip # 7 – Manage the Flow of Emotional Energy

Continue to monitor your feelings/emotions by periodically stopping a moment to recheck your *Emotional Indicator*. Any sign of negativity or resistance calls for immediate remedial action (**Allowing**).[B1, C6]

Dynamic Balance

When it comes to living on the earth plane, **there are no accidents. Everything has a purpose, and that purpose is soul evolution**. You are here to experience life in **all** its manifestations and to learn to **Balance the energies of** life to raise your consciousness and become the Master of your life.

- "There are no accidents in the human world. Everything is as it should be for each individual soul to learn their lessons. Many souls make it; many souls have to return [for] another incarnation to do so. It is choice, nothing more. It is the Self that creates the need by constantly berating and enforcing negative programming. When one can move to the Higher Self, one no longer has the problem." ~ Maitreya (Newsletter #83, September 1, 2003)

DYNAMIC BALANCE IS A PROCESS OF BECOMING

Some people choose to see ***Dynamic Balance*** as a set of beliefs and behaviors that one must adhere to or follow. I believe that any list of such requirements would necessarily be incomplete because each of us is on our own unique path. Each of us has our own unique lessons, karma, and past-life experiences to *balance*, and there is no single 'right' path to accomplish ***Allowing***, ***Balance***, and ***Alignment*** except the path that is 'right' for each of us individually.

I understand and believe that life is far less about ***what*** we do or ***how*** we do it and more about ***why*** we do it—motive and intention (character, integrity, etc.). Ultimately, it is about working toward ***vibrationally becoming*** through practicing the things that resonate with each of us individually as our own truth. The ultimate goal is ***Alignment*** with our own Higher Self, our direct connection with Source, Ultimate Being, God, All-That-Is, the Force, or whatever we individually choose to label that energy. But ultimate goals are about end-states. Getting to those end states is the process of becoming *aligned* with them. As I've said for many decades, "If you're looking for perfection, you are definitely on the wrong planet. That is why we are all here—together—on this third rock from the sun."

Dynamic Balance is the process of constant adjustment to constant change. But when we choose to put that change on 'pause' or 'hold' for whatever reason, the question of *balance* becomes moot because we are not *Allowing* the energy of Higher Self to flow through us naturally.

DYNAMIC BALANCE IS ACTIVE, NOT STATIC

Energy must be in motion or it is stagnant—'dead'—energy. On the earth plane at least, what is dead rots; it is poison. Dead energy in your etheric body translates to dead energy in your physical body, and that translates to physical pain, disease, and emotional dis-ease. Dead energy in your emotional or mental body produces the same results. Creation never ends and life is not static no matter how hard one might try to keep it from changing. Life is growth or it becomes death, and we have the choice to consciously incorporate that fact in our lives (***Dynamic Balance***) or choose to ignore it for the present in order to deal with it in some future incarnation. I will discuss the topic of change in more detail in a later chapter of *Dancing with the Energy*.[B3, C6]

DYNAMIC BALANCE IS LIVING IN THE NOW

Embracing the concept and practice of ***Dynamic Balance Allows*** us to be more open to accepting everything as *what IS* *without judgment,* conscious of how we *feel* in the moment, and choosing to respond responsibly and purposefully to both what is outside of us and what is inside of us right NOW.

Think about the following: the past is rife with feelings of guilt, resentment, anger, etc., all of which are negative energy. On the other hand, anxiety, worry, tension, and stress are all negative emotions regarding the future. That is not to say that we don't have negative emotions about the present, but at least we have the choice of doing something about them in the NOW. Dealing with negativity either from the past or in the future is fruitless. "What a waste of energy!" as Maitreya so often states.

And what about positive emotions at different points in time? Focusing your energies on pleasant memories of the past only exacerbates the implication that positive feelings cannot be experienced in the present. And focusing our present attention on positive emotions in the future? Well, that is the stuff of effective and efficient Manifesting![B3, C5] But that can only be done here and NOW. Waiting for the future to experience joy (or any positive emotion) is doomed to failure. The future *always* remains just that—the future. Creating a more desirable future—the life you want—can only be done *in the present*, the eternal NOW.

- "Do not dwell in the past, do not dream of the future, concentrate the mind on the present moment."
  ~ Gautama Buddha

What can one conclude from these perspectives? What does living in the NOW mean in practical terms? To put it simply, **Dynamic Balance is a state of non-attachment to whatever energy you are dealing with in the moment.** You have to learn to deal constructively with the energies of life *as you encounter*

Chapter 8: Understanding Conscious Living

and experience them in order to raise your consciousness and become the Master of your life. It is not something you put off to do tomorrow. ***It is following through on the decision to live each moment in conscious awareness of <u>what</u> you are doing and <u>why</u> you are doing it.*** It is being constantly aware of how you *feel* and then consciously choosing to ***adjust*** what you are thinking and doing NOW in order to *feel even better* both NOW and in the future.

THE IMPORTANCE OF DYNAMIC BALANCE

Why is ***Dynamic Balance*** so important? All planes of existence, and all souls, no matter their level of soul evolution, are aspects of the Creator, Source, Ultimate Being, God—whatever you are comfortable calling that energy. Even low-frequency vibrations are part of the Creator. For example, in the epic movie series, *Star Wars*, constant reference is made to '*the Force*' and (equally importantly) to '*the Dark Side of the Force*.' The point here is that <u>both</u> <u>sides</u> of the Force <u>are</u> the Force.

This is illustrated by the characters Anakin Skywalker and Darth Vader, in "*Episode III, Revenge of the Sith*" (2005). Misunderstanding the 'loss' of love (his wife) caused Anakin Skywalker to turn to the Dark Side and to assume the name and role of Darth Vader. His eventual understanding of what love is all about is what transforms Darth Vader back into Anakin Skywalker in "*Episode VI, Return of the Jedi*" (1983).

Another way of viewing this example is that <u>everything</u> is energy and <u>all</u> energy has value; it all comes from the same Source. It is all about how we choose to <u>use</u> the energy, not the energy itself. That is the key to understanding the concept of ***Dynamic Balance***.

DUALISM AND CONSCIOUS LIVING

The *dualistic thinking that is part of the illusion of the earth plane* leads us to think in terms of—and to talk about—opposite concepts such as high vs. low, good vs. bad, heaven vs. hell, God vs. Satan, etc. *All of these concepts are part of the earth-plane illusion.* What we label as the 'Dark Side of the Force' exists for one purpose: to expand our experience. It exists for our learning and soul evolution.

My teacher, Maitreya, talks about <u>unused</u> *energy* rather than <u>negative</u> *energy. Unused energy is just unexpressed energy.* Energy is just energy. It is neither positive nor negative; it just *IS*. Energy in motion is free and can manifest in constructive, positive ways when allowed to resonate or *Align* with 'the [Light Side of the] Force.' Unused energy is trapped, stagnant, and eventually manifests in undesirable ways corresponding to the 'Dark Side of the Force.' *Dynamic Balance* is a strategy for helping you to *detach* from the 'Dark Side' and *Allow* your *Alignment* with 'the [Light Side of the] Force.' It provides a framework for releasing and healing or transforming (*Balancing*) unused or trapped energy to restore and enhance *Allowing*, *Balancing*, and *Alignment* with Higher Self.

The illusion that life is all about the physical body and satisfying the insatiable desires of the ego versus 'spirituality' reflects only a shallow, surface understanding regarding both. In fact, 'life' is all about *learning to choose* opportunities to *grow* into a better version of yourself. The 'physical stuff' of the body and the ego are simply tools to enable this growth or spiritual transformation while the 'true you' (spirit, soul, whatever term resonates with your truth) is temporarily (and only partially) focused in the physical body.

So, how do you deal with this dualistic mentality? The perspective above has **Conscious Living** written all over it. *Conscious Living* gives you not only a blueprint, but also a practical approach to working toward **Alignment** (objective), **Balance** (strategy), and **Allowing** (tactics). **Dynamic Balance is at the heart of Conscious Living.**

Tips for Achieving Dynamic Balance

Dynamic Balance cannot be achieved without releasing, healing, or transforming trapped or unused energy. Previously, I presented a series of Tips for Dealing with Unused Energy.[B1, C7] For convenience, I'll repeat them here:

- Tip #1 – Check Your Emotional Indicator
- Tip #2 – Accept Your Subconscious Emotions
- Tip #3 – Understand Your Subconscious Emotions
- Tip #4 – Formulate a Conscious Intention
- Tip #5 – Clear Your Subconscious Emotions

Remember, many of your habits reflect trapped energy from the past and act as a brake to **Allowing** the energy to flow unhindered. Since this is so important, you may want to review the Tips for Changing Your Habits in the previous chapter.

Also remember that there are no accidents. If you are to truly accept and understand what happens to you in your life, the answer is always within. There are *always* lessons involved[B2, C3], there may be karma as well[B2, C4], and more likely than not these will come forth into your current life as past-life energy and 'unfinished business.'[B2, C5] Their purpose is to help you to grow in **Allowing, Balancing,** and **Aligning** your life energies with your Higher Self.

Learn to accept the positive and the negative in life *without judgment*. In other words, learn to detach from the negative emotional energy of life. What IS just IS. You can't blame anyone, including yourself. *Blame is a form of judgment. The key to Dynamic Balance is detaching from negative emotions and beliefs* (either from this life or from past lives) that you are still holding-on to, thereby preventing you from growing and raising your consciousness. This also gives other people in your life a chance to release their emotions, which helps them. (Spiritually-oriented people not only work on themselves, they often serve as instruments for Spirit to work on others as well.)

- "Let go of the emotions and the emotional body and you can fly! That is how you can raise your vibration."
  ~ Maitreya (Newsletter #277, January 6, 2010)

You will find meditation to be an important contributor to *Dynamic Balance* primarily because it is incredibly helpful in *learning to live in the present moment without judgment and without attachment to outside energies. This is the core of Dynamic Balance*. A daily practice of meditation helps to *train you to maintain the Alpha State of consciousness a greater proportion of the time while going about your daily routine*. Because the Alpha State is such an important topic, I will discuss it later in greater detail.[B3, C4]

In essence, this means living each moment as if you rarely leave the Alpha State. It is taking this state of consciousness (*Conscious Living*—which includes non-attachment to the emotional body and living in the moment) into everyday life, not just sitting in the silence of formal meditation practice. It is not an escape from life but rather experiencing *with presence all* of life in *all* its fullness with every breath. This state of "Presence" Eckhart Tolle (1948–; spiritual teacher, motivational speaker, and author) speaks of is very similar to "Mindfulness" as taught by Thich Nhat Hanh (1926–; Vietnamese Buddhist monk and peace activist).

In short, *consciously choosing* to take an expanded state of *non-attached awareness* into the 'now' of your daily activities is the key to both ***Dynamic Balance*** and to ***Conscious Living*** (awareness, choice, and non-judgment).

How does one do that? Well, learning to live more in the Alpha State[B3, C4] is a wonderful training ground and practice for 'presence,' 'mindfulness,' 'walking meditation,' '***Dynamic Balance***'—whatever term best resonates with *you*. But at some point, the 'rubber hits the road' in terms of actually doing it. Here is one simple and effective way to get started:

- Whatever you are doing in your daily activities (for example, walking down the street, washing your hands, eating lunch)—whatever, ***stop suddenly.***

- Just be present to what is going on within and around you for 30 seconds. Then resume what you were doing.

- Do this at least six times a day. More is okay, but not less than six times. That is a total of 3 minutes (minimum) each day.

This will likely take a little bit of extra work (attention) until it becomes a habit, but as you become accustomed to doing it you will find that just ***suddenly becoming present*** changes the energy of whatever you are doing.

No matter what else you do, learn to be at peace in the company of your own thoughts. Earlier in this book I dealt with consciously monitoring your emotions. Learn to do the same thing with your thoughts. Listen to them. Consciously try to

Align your thoughts with your Higher Self. Until you become adept at 'tuning out' the noise of your environment at will (being actively aware of it but not involved in it—'*in* the world but not *of* the world'), you can't really learn to tune out the chatter of the Self which constantly plays a running theme of negativity, fear, and doubt. There is an old saying, "Silence is golden." This applies not only to the tendency to speak before thinking, but it applies especially to the tendency to get too involved in the mind chatter of the Self. Listening to the 'silence'—especially *between* thoughts—is a very effective way of learning to develop the 'presence' of pure consciousness. When it comes to **Dynamic Balance**, silence really *is* golden. There is nothing more important to the attainment of both **Dynamic Balance** and of **Conscious Living** than learning to 'listen to the silence' (*your* intuition) as you proceed throughout your daily routine.

Summary of Tips for Conscious Living

GENERAL TIPS FOR CONSCIOUS LIVING

- Tip #1 – Refine Your Awareness of Every Situation
- Tip #2 – Take Responsibility for Your Choices
- Tip #3 – Avoid Judging Yourself and Others
- Tip #4 – Check Your Emotional Indicator
- Tip #5 – Choose a Thought That Feels a Little Better
- Tip #6 – Take <u>Vibrational</u> Action <u>First</u>
- Tip #7 – Manage the Flow of Emotional Energy

Concluding Comments

The Foundations of Conscious Living in Book 1 of ***Dancing with the Energy*** are the foundational principles—the basic tools and raw materials which are the building blocks of your daily life. You now have at your disposal an understanding of these tools for improving the quality of your life here and now, as well as for raising your vibration and working toward becoming the Master of your life.

To a very great extent, ***Conscious Living*** involves learning about and working with the subconscious mind to ***Allow*** your energies to flow freely in order to ***Balance*** those energies for the purpose of ***Aligning*** them with your Higher Self. As the seat of soul memory, the subconscious mind takes center stage in understanding and using *The Foundations of Conscious Living*.

The foundations discussed in this book are essential for understanding and overcoming the limiting factors of your life which are the basis of *Book 2: Conscious Living — What's Holding You Back?* Book 2 also includes Tips for using those fundamental tools to assist you in making progress toward—and ultimately achieving—your life goals.

Book 3 of the *Dancing with the Energy* series deals with *Conscious Living—Creating the Life You Desire*. In it you will learn how to use and apply the tools and techniques (in addition to those in Books 1 and 2) for the purpose of creating that life and simultaneously raising your vibration.

The Contents of Books 2 and 3 are listed on the following page for your convenience.

Dancing with the Energy

Contents of Book 2:
Conscious Living — What's Holding You Back?

Introduction to Book 2
Chapter 1: Conscious Living and Your Life Energies
Chapter 2: Spiritual Astrology
Chapter 3: Learning Life Lessons
Chapter 4: Balancing Your Karmic Obligations
Chapter 5: Releasing Past-Life Energy
Chapter 6: Conscious Living: Healing Your Life Energies
Concluding Comments
Appendix A: Inspirational and Educational Resources

Contents of Book 3:
Conscious Living — Creating the Life You Desire

Introduction to Book 3
Chapter 1: Working Through the Energy
Chapter 2: Health, Well-Being, and Energy Healing
Chapter 3: Making Your Affirmations Work!
Chapter 4: Gifts of the Alpha State
Chapter 5: Secrets of Manifesting
Chapter 6: Dancing with the Energy
Chapter 7: Conscious Living: Concluding Comments
Appendix A: Inspirational and Educational Resources

Appendix A: Inspirational and Educational Resources

—A—

Abraham-Hicks (*A New Beginning, Volume 1*, 1987)

Abraham-Hicks (*Ask and It Is Given: Learning to Manifest Your Desires*, 2004)

Abraham-Hicks (*Getting into the Vortex Guided Meditation CD and User Guide*, 2010)

Abraham-Hicks (*Money and the Law of Attraction: Learning to Attract Health, Wealth and Happiness*, 2008)

Abraham-Hicks (*The Law of Attraction; The Basics of the Teachings of Abraham*, 2006)

Abraham-Hicks (*The Vortex, Where the Law of Attraction Assembles All Cooperative Relationships*, 2009)

Allen, James (*As A Man Thinketh*, 1903)

Austen, Jane (*Sense and Sensibility*, 1811)

Dancing with the Energy: Book 1
The Foundations of Conscious Living

—B—

Bohr, Niels (*Essays 1932-1957 on Atomic Physics and Human Knowledge*, 1958)

Braden, Gregg *(The Divine Matrix: Bridging Time, Space, Miracles, and Belief*, 2007)

—D—

Dyer, Dr. Wayne W. (*The Power of Intention*, 2004)

Dyer, Dr. Wayne W. (*You'll See It When You Believe It*, 2009)

—G—

Goswami, PhD, Amit (*Physics of the Soul: The Quantum Book of Living, Dying, Reincarnation, and Immortality*, 2004)

Goswami, PhD, Amit (*The Everything Answer Book: How Quantum Science Explains Love, Death, and the Meaning of Life*, 2017)

—H—

Hill, Napoleon (*Think and Grow Rich*, 1937)

—M—

Maitreya Speaks Volume I (2012, Channeled by Margaret McElroy, www.Maitreya.co)

Maitreya Speaks Volume II (2012, Channeled by Margaret McElroy, www.Maitreya.co)

Maitreya Speaks Volume III (2012, Channeled by Margaret McElroy, www.Maitreya.co)

Appendix A: Inspirational and Educational Resources

Maitreya Speaks Volume IV (2012, Channeled by Margaret McElroy, www.Maitreya.co)

—S—

Sheldrake, Rupert (*The Presence of the Past*, 1988)

—W—

Walters, J. Donald (*Awaken To Superconsciousness*, 2000)

Walters, J. Donald (*The Path*, 2004)

—Y—

Yogananda, Paramhansa (*Autobiography of a Yogi*, 1946)

Milton Keynes UK
Ingram Content Group UK Ltd.
UKHW011045131123
432477UK00001B/94